pray

a word a day

pray
a word a day

Connecting with God One Word at a Time

editors of guideposts

Pray a Word a Day

Published by Guideposts Books & Inspirational Media
100 Reserve Road, Suite E200
Danbury, CT 06810
Guideposts.org

Acknowledgments

Every attempt has been made to credit the sources of copyrighted material used in this book. If any such acknowledgment has been inadvertently omitted or miscredited, receipt of such information would be appreciated.

Scripture quotations marked (CEV) are taken from *Holy Bible: Contemporary English Version.* Copyright © 1995 American Bible Society.

Scripture quotations marked (ESV) are taken from the *Holy Bible, English Standard Version.* Copyright © 2001 by Crossway Bibles, a division of Good News Publishers. Used by permission. All rights reserved.

Scripture quotations marked (GW) are taken from *GOD'S WORD Translation.* Copyright © 1995 by God's Word to the Nations. Used by permission of Baker Publishing Group.

Scripture quotations marked (KJV) are taken from the *King James Version of the Bible.* (Public domain.)

Scripture quotations marked (MSG) are taken from *The Message.* Copyright © 1993, 1994, 1995, 1996, 2000, 2001, 2002 by Eugene H. Peterson.

Scripture quotations marked (NASB) are taken from the *New American Standard Bible.* Copyright © 1960, 1962, 1963, 1968, 1971, 1972, 1973, 1975, 1977, 1995 by The Lockman Foundation, La Habra, California. Used by permission.

Scripture quotations marked (NHEB) are taken from the *New Heart English Bible* (Public domain.)

Scripture quotations marked (NIRV) are taken from *The Holy Bible, New International Reader's Version.* Copyright © 1996 by Biblica, Inc. Used by permission of Zondervan. All rights reserved worldwide. zondervan.com

Scripture quotations marked (NIV) are taken from *The Holy Bible, New International Version.* Copyright © 1973, 1978, 1984, 2011 by Biblica, Inc. Used by permission of Zondervan. All rights reserved worldwide. zondervan.com

Scripture quotations marked (NKJV) are taken from *The Holy Bible, New King James Version.* Copyright © 1982 by Thomas Nelson.

Scripture quotations marked (NLT) are from the *Holy Bible, New Living Translation.* Copyright © 1996, 2004, 2007 by Tyndale House Foundation. Used by permission of Tyndale House Publishers Inc., Carol Stream, Illinois. All rights reserved.

Scripture quotations marked (NRSV) are taken from the *New Revised Standard Version Bible.* Copyright © 1989 by the Division of Christian Education of the National Council of the Churches of Christ in the United States of America. Used by permission. All rights reserved.

Scripture quotations marked (TLB) are taken from *The Living Bible.* Copyright © 1971 by Tyndale House Publishers, Inc., Carol Stream, Illinois. All rights reserved.

Scripture quotations marked (TPT) are taken from *The Passion Translation.* Copyright © 2016 by Broadstreet Publishing Group, Savage, Minnesota. All rights reserved.

Scriptures quotations marked (VOICE) are taken from the THE VOICE (The Voice): Scripture taken from THE VOICE™. Copyright© 2008 by Ecclesia Bible Society. All rights reserved.

Cover design by Serena Fox, Serena Fox Design Company
Interior design by Serena Fox, Serena Fox Design Company
Cover photo by TK
Typeset by Aptara, Inc.

Printed and bound in the United States of America
10 9 8 7 6 5 4 3 2 1

Prayer is the exercise of drawing on the grace of God.

—*Oswald Chambers*

Introduction

Devote yourselves to prayer with an alert mind and a thankful heart. Colossians 4:2 NLT

Welcome to *Pray a Word a Day*, a nondated, 365-day devotional that encourages you to be intentional about connecting with God by focusing on a different word each day. Journey through a land-scape of words of all kinds—words that will inspire, comfort, and challenge you, or put a smile on your face. Each day's entry starts with an inspirational quote or Scripture centered on a simple everyday word. A short true story and a prayer follow, motivating you to see God at work in that word. As you "carry" the word with you throughout the day and reflect on it, you will be surprised to see how God is working in your life in big or small ways. Will you encounter the word on a billboard, in an email, or in a conver-sation? Whose voice is God using to speak to you? This book is filled with a bounty of 365 unique words for you to meditate on and ponder as you enjoy your prayer time and sip your coffee. But each featured word may also be used as a powerful tool to invite others, family members, friends, and neighbors to unite in prayer by focusing on the same word. Each day's entry will take just a minute or two to read, and at the bottom of each page there's space for you to jot down your experiences and thoughts. This little log is a marvelous reminder of how persistently and sweetly God is reaching out to you all the time.

As you make your way through *Pray a Word a Day*, you will be amazed by God's powerful impact on your life and on your relation-ship with Him as you connect with Him day by day, word by word.

Faithfully yours,
Editors of Guideposts

goodness

Surely goodness and mercy shall follow me all the days of
my life: and I will dwell in the house of the Lᴏʀᴅ forever.
—Psalm 23:6 KJV

When I was a little girl, this verse made me very
nervous. I thought there were two little old ladies,
Shirley Goodness and her friend Mercy, who were
going to follow me everywhere!

Imagine my relief when I learned my mistake. Years later I
learned that the original Hebrew word translated as "follow"
really means "chase." Sometimes when I'm feeling sorry for
myself, or when I'm unable to forgive myself for a wrongdoing, I
think about being "chased" by goodness and mercy. God loves
me so much that He sends them out to pursue me. He is merciful toward me when I am not merciful toward myself; He sends
goodness to me and instructs it to hurry up!

—Michelle

*Thank You, Lord, for sending Your goodness to me—for pursuing
me with Your mercy. Amen.*

change

Change your thoughts and you change your world.
—Norman Vincent Peale

Recently, the word of the day suggested by my Bible reading was "change." So I prayed that short word throughout the day: "Change my heart, O God. Give me strength and hope through the changes of these coming weeks." A grocery-store transaction put change in my pocket, prompting a prayer for the wise use of our "loose change." A sudden schedule change seemed providential. And so on.

Even Facebook somehow got into the act. I know Facebook's algorithms detect websites I visit or purchases I make and incorporate those into ads and promotions, but I couldn't think of any online hint I gave of my word-of-the-day prayer. But "change" nonetheless became a theme, popping onto my computer screen through the rest of the day. I even noticed the word in a television commercial or two, which sent me back to prayer when I saw and heard it.

—Bob

Father, change my heart, thoughts, life,
and circumstances as You will. Amen.

together

None of us, including me, ever do great things.
But we can all do small things with great love,
and together we can do something wonderful.
—Mother Teresa

This past year I have become involved in a ministry that gives baby showers for new refugee moms here in Boise, Idaho. Refugees are brave. Leaving family and friends and flying halfway around the world to establish a new life is daunting. If I can be part of making that transition easier, I want in. All over this world, millions of people need food, water, and shelter. Diapers too. Such needs can be completely overwhelming, until I remind myself of all the people who are working together to usher in love and hope. *Together* is a powerful concept. I may not have a whole lot to offer on my own, but together, little by little, small things can be accomplished with great love.

—Susanna

*Lord, show me how to work together with those around me
in the spirit of Your love. Amen.*

enlarge

Jabez cried out to the God of Israel, "Oh, that you would
bless me and enlarge my territory!"
—1 Chronicles 4:10 NIV

Two of my grandchildren cope daily with a condition known as cystic fibrosis, which affects (among other things) their breathing and lung capacity. They undergo treatments a couple times each day to try to maintain—and enlarge—their pulmonary functions. So, I pray every day for such results, sometimes with the single word "Enlarge."

It's a great word to pray, and it can apply to so many areas of concern and desire. For God's kingdom to rule in my life: Enlarge. For my capacity to love others: Enlarge. For my ability to give generously: Enlarge. For the church's influence in my community: Enlarge. For the ability to see clearly, speak con-structively, and work creatively: Enlarge.

—Bob

Lord, I pray that You would bless me and enlarge my territory.
Amen.

creativity

Creativity is intelligence having fun.
—Albert Einstein

When I taught sixth grade, I papered the classroom with colorful posters featuring inspirational quotes. Then I had my students complete a quote walk, studying each poster, choosing their favorite. One funny class favorite was a fake Abraham Lincoln quote, "Don't believe everything you read on the Internet just because there's a picture with a quote next to it." Another was Albert Einstein's real quote, "Creativity is intelligence having fun."

With kids, creativity is a given. Everyone likes to have fun. Our minds and hands are naturally drawn to build, craft, and problem-solve. *Why?* We are made in the Creator's image, the One Who spoke galaxies into existence with a single word. When I write a poem, plant flowers, or prepare a delicious meal, God's presence and creativity are unleashed in me. What could be more fun than that?

—Susanna

God, thank You for unleashing Your creativity in my life. Touch those around me with the creative gifts You have given me.
Amen.

persistence

He may not get up and give you the bread, just
because you are his friend. But he will get up and give
you as much as you need, simply because you are not
ashamed to keep on asking.
—Luke 11:8 CEV

Really? He's playing the piano with only one hand?" My
husband, Kevin, smiled at my response to the recording
of a well-known twentieth-century Austrian pianist Paul
Wittgenstein. I marveled at the depth of feeling and wide use
of the keyboard in this composition.

Wittgenstein lost his right arm during World War I. In a
Siberian prison camp, he determined to continue his career
after the war by commissioning music written for the left hand.
Many of Wittgenstein's arrangements are performed by modern pianists—even two-handed ones. Thanks to his persistence,
music lovers on every continent find joy and inspiration. All
because a one-armed pianist refused to give up.

—Jeanette

*Lord, may I persist in every good desire, remembering
that nothing is impossible with You. Amen.*

giving

Every good and perfect gift is from above.
—James 1:17 NIV

Mom had been battling breast cancer that had spread to her bones when she became confused and disoriented. As the ambulance lifted her from the sofa onto the gurney, the nurse in me knew her cancer had gone to her brain as well. My eyes took in the woven basket Mom always kept nearby. It was filled with pretty note cards she loved to send to cheer anyone she thought of while she rested. The wooden spring clothespins she used to attach them to her old wrought-iron mailbox were there as well. But then I noticed something else. The unaddressed envelopes already bore Mom's Love stamps, ready to dispatch at a moment's notice. My mother would never pen another encouraging missive in this life. But she'd sent one more message to my heart: the importance of always being ready to give.

—Roberta

Lord, teach me to give in ways large and small,
every single day. Amen.

never

Never give up, for that is just the place
and time that the tide will turn.
—Harriet Beecher Stowe

Desperation prompted my first prayer retreat. My teenage son was struggling and seemed to have abandoned his faith. My wife and I were burdened and concerned for him. So I went to a retreat center for three days, determined to pray for him like I'd never prayed before. Much of my praying those three days focused on God's "never" promises: to never leave (Deut. 31:6), never forsake (Heb. 13:5), never break covenant (Judg. 2:1), never let the righteous be shaken (Ps. 55:22), never forget me (Isa. 49:15), never let His words fail (Mark 13:31), never let me—or my son—go (John 10:28).

God answered my prayers. Not immediately, but abundantly and overwhelmingly. Since then, I occasionally return to "never" prayers, reminding myself of God's faithfulness to His promises.

—Bob

*God, You never give up on me; let me never give up on You.
Amen.*

learn

The mind that is not baffled is not employed.
—Wendell Berry

When my children were school-age, we had the "What did you learn today?" conversation around the supper table almost every night. "Nothing" wasn't an acceptable answer, so they were usually prepared. Zero times anything is zero. If you step on the line in basketball, you're out of bounds...and lots of other stuff, equally as entertaining.

The kids grew up and flew the nest, my husband and I divorced, and supper became eerily quiet. Boring. Most of all, lonely. Until I started asking myself, "What did I learn today?" It was hard to answer at first, until I started paying attention. I learned how to check the air pressure in my tires. The names of my new neighbors. Most of all, I learn anew every day how God's love goes with me, no matter my circumstances.

—Jennie

Lord, keep my mind ever curious to learn new things. Amen.

partnership

Two are better than one, because they have a
good reward for their toil.
—Ecclesiastes 4:9 ESV

A few years ago, my wife brought home an eight-pound mini pinscher/Chihuahua mix (known as a Chipin) named Nina. She settled in immediately, lazing on the couch and helping herself to any available food.

Nina's arrival came as a shock to our black lab, Nick. Despite the nice alliteration of their names, Nick and Nina did not like each other. They competed over food, attention, and napping spots.

One day, Nick was outside chasing his longtime nemesis, a particularly sly squirrel. Usually he'd chase the squirrel underneath the shed and that would be it. That changed as Nina raced behind Nick, squeezing underneath the shed and flushing the squirrel out. The squirrel escaped up a tree, but Nick had a newfound appreciation for Nina. Like Nick, I know the value of partnership, and I love seeing it work in unlikely ways.

—John

Lord, help me to seek partnership, even when I do not see how.
Amen.

holy

Make me want again to be holy.
—Thomas Merton

Years ago, I discovered The Abbey of Gethsemani, a Trappist monastery in the western Kentucky hills, where the monks and their guests maintain silence day and night. I've entered the chapel at the monastery hundreds of times, often joining the monks for their prayers, held seven times every day, seven days a week, fifty-two weeks a year. Whatever else is on my mind or in my heart before arriving, a sense of the holy soon pervades my spirit, and I "Go near to listen rather than to offer the sacrifice of fools" (Eccles. 5:1 NIV). After each visit, I've tried (with varying degrees of success) to let God's holy presence rule my heart, mind, and conduct. As Moses discovered in the burning bush and Elijah in the cleft of the rock, where God dwells, holiness reigns.

—Bob

God, fill me and my life with Your holy presence. Amen.

beloved

Beloved, let us love one another, for love is of God; and everyone who loves is born of God and knows God.
—1 John 4:7 NKJV

'd just had a disagreement with a loved one and sat alone, stewing on the couch. My pulse raced and my thoughts scattered as I justified my side of the argument to myself. An hour passed and still I remained in that spot. But as the afternoon wore on, winning and being "right" seemed less and less important. What mattered was making amends. My heart ached as I prayed for guidance.

When my beloved and I exchanged apologies, the words I remember most were, "I love you and always will." The very words God spoke in my heart as I prayed.

—Heidi

Lord, help me grow closer to You as I share my love with others. Amen.

bloom

Bloom in all Thy beauty in the garden of my heart.
—Sidney Cox

My mother, who died when I was fourteen, was a masterful pianist who played regularly for our church services. A favorite chorus of hers—and, subsequently, mine—was one written by a family friend, which referred to Jesus as "lily of the valley," followed by the petition, "bloom in all Thy beauty in the garden of my heart."

It's a sweet prayer I repeat often, for myself and for my family—sometimes by singing those words and sometimes with the one-word prayer "Bloom." I want the beauty and fragrance of Jesus's presence to be seen in my life, my face, my words, and my actions, and to see it bloom in those I love.

—Bob

Jesus, Jesus, Lily of the Valley, "bloom in all Thy beauty in the garden of my heart." Amen.

tree

At least there is hope for a tree:
if it is cut down, it will sprout again.
—Job 14:7 NIV

A lush weeping willow tree overlooks the pond behind our house. Long, green fronds droop from the top to the ground below. Three winters after we planted it, an ice storm ravaged its tender branches. When spring arrived, no green appeared on them. By summer, we decided to cut down the tree. I was heartsick. Another winter came, followed by a new spring. And there, next to the stump of the original tree, a new sprout appeared—flimsy and fragile but boasting green buds.

That sprout is now a strong, solid trunk that supports healthy, graceful branches. Every morning as I gaze through my kitchen window at the willow tree, I am reminded of its resilience. Against the odds, a single sprout was determined to rise up and thrive, and it did.

—Karen

Father, when I feel defeated, You give me hope,
like a damaged tree that sprouts again. Amen.

sleep

God gave us sleep to remind us we are not him.
—Charles Spurgeon

'''ve always been a night owl. I can easily stay up until one
or two in the morning, go to bed, and get up a few hours
later to start my day. But I know that habit is not a good
one. I'm tired most days—and no wonder. Numerous studies
have shown the importance of sleep. When I do snag six or
seven hours of shut-eye, I wake up feeling like a million bucks.
Sometimes I can't sleep because worries and concerns overtake
my mind. That's when I ask the Lord to calm my spirit so that
I can get the rest I need. I once heard a pastor say we should
give our worries to God and go to sleep—He's going to be up
all night anyway. Best. Advice. Ever.

—Barbranda

*Lord, please grant me the sleep I need each night
to rejuvenate my mind, body, and spirit. Amen.*

innovation

Creativity is thinking up new things. Innovation
is doing new things.
—Theodore Leavitt

My older sister Jenny was born with cerebral palsy, a condition that left her with very little muscle control and confined to a wheelchair. Despite not being able to speak words, Jenny had an incredible ability to communicate with her smiles and her eyes. My mom was the best at interpreting what Jenny was saying.

Jenny's special needs made even a simple task like dressing to go out for the day a time-consuming, tricky challenge. If a jacket didn't work for Jenny, Mom would innovate—removing zippers and buttons and using Velcro closures in their place. Mom used that same Velcro to create a safety harness that kept Jenny from falling out of her wheelchair.

Just as Jenny communicated her love to us in different ways, Mom's innovations with Velcro made Jenny feel loved—and warm!

—John

Lord, help me to innovate out of love, to use Your gifts of reason and insight to help me find new ways to serve in Your name. Amen.

abundance

Life in abundance comes only through great love.
—Elbert Hubbard

My grandfather liked to brag that all his kids helped people: One son became a psychologist, the other a teacher, and my mom, a nurse. My two aunts were also teachers, so I was aware from an early age that there's an abundance of good people in the world. It's been delightful and inspiring to meet more as I travel through life. Civilians who write to soldiers they've never met. Subway passengers who reach out to a fellow traveler in need of directions. Friends who travel hundreds of miles for a short visit. They all serve as reminders of abundant kindness.

—Allison

Lord, I've been blessed to experience an abundance of good throughout Your creation. I pray that all Your children get to see the best in one another. Amen.

quiet

Quiet! Be still!
—Mark 4:39 NIV

To be in Israel on Yom HaShoah, the day each year that commemorates the lives lost in the Holocaust, is unforgettable. At 10:00 a.m., a siren sounds. Drivers exit their cars, shopkeepers step outside, schoolchildren stand by their desks, and for two minutes, everything stops. An entire nation quiets itself.

One day a furious storm arose as Jesus and His closest followers sailed on the Sea of Galilee, but Jesus slept through it. His panicked followers awakened Him. The Bible says, "He got up, rebuked the wind and said to the waves, 'Quiet! Be still!' Then the wind died down and it was completely calm" (Mark 4:39 NIV).

I may not command winds and waves, but I can say "Quiet." It may be a plea to God. It may be a command to my own mind and heart. Either way, it's a path to peace and calm.

—Bob

Jesus, interrupt the noise of this day with moments of quiet. Amen.

read

Anything worth reading is worth reading slowly.
—Johnny Uzan

'm a to-do list kind of person. Whether my tasks consist of exercise, housework, or even FaceTiming my grandkids, I like to jot them down and then cross them off my list. The same is true for reading. I write down my reading goals for the coming months and assign each a block of time. I read news. Poetry. Essays. Fiction. And, yeah, I allow myself a little time each day to scroll through Facebook.

The Bible is on my list too. I recently completed a "Read the Bible in One Year" challenge and felt very self-satisfied. Until I realized how little I'd truly absorbed. When I fly through the latest best seller without letting it soak in, it doesn't much matter. But when I read the Bible, I must remind myself not to hurry. God's Holy Word is not something to scratch off my list.

—Jennie

*Slow me down, Lord, so that I may learn the lessons
Your book teaches. Amen.*

patience

Have courage for the great sorrows of life and patience
for the small ones; and when you have laboriously
accomplished your daily task, go to sleep in peace.
God is awake.
—Victor Hugo

P atience isn't an innate virtue for me. Almost everything I've learned about patience has come from the animals in my life, especially dogs. My current animal pal, Cody, an adolescent, seventy-pound, mixed-breed rescue with a bad attitude, required a lifetime's worth of patience in our early days together. Mine was his sixth home in nine months, and to say that Cody didn't trust people is a huge understatement. But every time I met his resistance with my patience, he took another step toward becoming the well-adjusted, devoted companion he is today.

—Julie

Dear God, thank You for all the lessons in patience You have given me. I could use a few more for the times ahead. And since I'm not always easy to deal with, please encourage patience in my loved ones too. Amen.

pray

God is looking for people to use, and if you can get usable, he will wear you out. The most dangerous prayer you can pray is this: "Use me."
—Rick Warren

One day, my friend shared with me and another church member her concerns about her mother's health and the challenges she faced as a caregiver. We listened patiently and sympathized with her. I was prepared to give my usual response, "You'll be in my prayers." But this time, different words immediately came out of my mouth: "Let's pray right now."

"Yes," my other friend said. "Let's pray."

The three of us held hands and right on the spot I offered a prayer, asking God to help and give direction. After we said "Amen," my friend thanked us. Because of that day years ago, I learned it's better to pray with someone immediately rather than wait until later. God hears us anytime, anywhere.

—Barbranda

Dear God, use me to stop and pray for others immediately when they need help. Amen.

twist

God has a surprise for you.
—Luke 1:30 MSG

A long the wooded path, I stopped by a funny-looking plant with two giant, droopy leaves; it looked almost like a green umbrella. My biologist brother called it a *mayapple*. "Take a peek under the leaves," he said. I dropped to my knees, rested my head on the moist soil, and twisted my neck to gaze up. There beneath the leaves, a single snow-white flower stared back at me. What a beauty-in-hiding! And I almost missed it. Without an awkward position and a twist, I would have continued along the path and never known it existed. What else have I missed, below, above, or behind something else? Today I'm going to stop and twist to find other surprises God has for me.

—Becky

God, help me discover Your handiwork, not only in obvious places but also in hidden ones. Amen.

always

Command the children of Israel, that they bring thee pure oil olive beaten for the light, to cause the lamp to burn always.
—Exodus 27:20 KJV

My children remember our family trip to the Washington, DC, area for the "millions of miles" their mother and I made them walk—or so they claim. One vivid memory for me was a visit to President John F. Kennedy's grave in Arlington National Cemetery, in Virginia, where an "eternal flame" burns. It's a moving, memorable sight.

When God gave instructions for building the tabernacle in the wilderness, He commanded for "the lamp to burn always." It reminds me of the old song with the line, "Give me oil in my lamp, keep me burning." That's my prayer, for me and those I love: for the lamp of my faith, fervor, devotion, and delight in God "to burn always." No flameout. No burnout. Not so much as a flicker.

—Bob

Lord, fuel the flames of my life and love for You—always. Amen.

victory

Start where you are. Use what you have. Do what you can.
—Arthur Ashe

Things looked bleak for our indoor professional soccer team. We'd been losing. We were on the road facing one of the league's strongest teams—a team that had been extremely tough when we played them at our home field. They had the league's highest home arena attendance, with crowds of loud, boisterous, fiercely loyal fans. Our top goal scorer, an all-star and one of the league's leading goal scorers, was injured and unavailable. And to kick in a little something extra, the match would be the nationally televised "Game of the Week."

We had two choices. We could view the circumstances as insurmountable, play halfheartedly, yield to the pressure, and just accept the expected loss. Or we could resolve together that victory was still possible. We played "lights out," fighting until the final whistle, and left the arena with a 7–5 victory.

—Steve

Lord, remind me that the first steps toward victory, in any aspect of life, are showing up and competing. Amen.

feathers

He will cover you with his feathers, and under his wings you will find refuge; his faithfulness will be your shield and rampart.
—Psalm 91:4 NIV

My three boys like to show me pictures and videos of animals with their babies. They know it thrills my mama heart. One picture featured a beautiful, orange-breasted bird sitting on a branch, with a protective wing encircling each of her two downy babies. The baby birds looked completely content tucked beneath her cozy feathers. Their mom's wings kept them safe from the elements.

Just as that mama bird protected her babies with her feathers, God protects me from life's harsh elements. When I shelter under His wings, every difficult situation, heartache or anxiety is filtered through His feathers. His care. His love. His provision. His forgiveness. His mercy. His guidance. In His protective care, covered by His feathers, I am content.

—Susanna

God, thank You for Your sheltering care and encircling care. Cover me with Your feathers today. Amen.

charm

Charm is deceptive, and beauty is fleeting; but a woman
who fears the LORD is to be praised.
—Proverbs 31:30 NIV

When I was young, Tillie, a woman at my church, gave me the first novel I ever read. Tillie was a teacher, and I loved her passion for learning and her endearing ways.

When Tillie got up in years and was downsizing her home library, she offered me the first pick of her extensive book collection. Not long after that, Tillie moved to a care home. How I dreaded visiting her away from the place she loved. I steeled myself for a sad woman whose body told of the passage of time. But when I entered Tillie's room, she was dressed in a chic pair of slacks and a turtleneck top. She flashed me a brilliant smile that belied nine decades of living. "Roberta!" she said. "I'm *so* glad God brought us together today."

—Roberta

A woman who fears and reveres You, Lord?
Help me be like her. Amen.

kiss

Greet one another with a kiss of love.
—1 Peter 5:14 NKJV

Turning thirteen was hard on my daughter Meg. It was hard on me too. With hormones raging, she argued about things that had never caused a ripple before. Chores. Homework. Friends. Even what we were having for dinner.

"You just don't understand!" Meg would say whenever I insisted that she do—or not do—something. "My life is so hard!" It was almost impossible not to laugh. But laughing, of course, just made things worse. She would roll her eyes when I told her I understood because I'd been thirteen once myself. Sometimes, she would get nose to nose with me and argue through clenched teeth. On one such occasion, I had an idea. Rather than argue back through my own clenched teeth, I tilted my head and kissed her on the cheek.

You know what? She kissed me back. Peace restored, at least for a while.

—Jennie

Lord, remind me always of Your commandment:
Love one another. Amen.

memory

Memory is the scribe of the soul.
—Aristotle

A device connected to our television uses multiple apps to watch events, shows, and movies. It also allows us to use our family photos as a screensaver on the television. Sometimes we'll spend time watching the photos stream by rather than turning on a show, and frequently the photos will jog our memory of a long-forgotten occasion—or a deceased friend or family member.

Our Jewish friends use a phrase to refer to someone who has died: "May his [or her] memory be for a blessing." Sometimes it's shortened to "of blessed memory." I think of it often, as I am blessed by the memory of someone who was—and continues to be—important in my life. The memory forms a prayer of sorts. And a reminder to live today in such a way that my memory will be a blessing.

—Bob

Eternal One, thank You for so many people whose memories are a blessing to me. Amen.

grow

Consider how the wild flowers grow...not even Solomon in all
his splendor was dressed like one of these.
—Luke 12:27 NIV

Nothing brightens a dining table like a bouquet of flowers. And, yes, roses in an elegant crystal vase are lovely.
But no lovelier than the "ditch flowers" that grow in
profusion along the rural roadsides where I live. Ox-eye daisies.
Purple clover. Queen Anne's lace. Honeysuckle. Thistle. Black-
eyed Susans. Trumpet vine.

From early spring until first frost, I keep a pair of scissors and
a jug of water in my car and frequently pull off the road to snip
fistfuls of whatever flowering treasures I've spotted. At home,
I arrange them willy-nilly in quart-sized canning jars. One of
the jars adorns my own table. The rest I give to neighbors and
friends, because a bouquet of wildflowers always brings a smile.

Even Solomon himself was not dressed as splendidly.

—Jennie

*Thank You, Lord, for the amazing beauty You've planted
all around us. Amen.*

commitment

Commitment is what transforms a promise into reality.
—Abraham Lincoln

could think of a million things I would have rather been doing that Saturday than spending the day building a wheelchair ramp, a commitment I volunteer for every month. Especially on this cold blustery day. My muscles ached from hours on my knees, screwing together pieces of a wood frame. *Why do I do this?* I wondered. It was near dusk by the time we were finished. The homeowner wheeled himself onto the ramp to inspect our work. "This is life changing for me," he said. "I don't know how to thank you." Once again, I learned the value of commitment, of following through, of showing up for people—even when I don't want to—just as my Father in heaven is committed to being there for me.

—Evan

Lord, help me to follow through on my commitments,
even when it's difficult. Amen.

broken

I will...bind up the broken.
—Ezekiel 34:16 NASB

My mother once gave me a porcelain figurine of a woman surrounded by her young children, saying, "You're such a good mother." I treasured it. Years later I packed it carefully when we moved to Alaska. My mistake was setting it in the center of the kitchen table when we unpacked. My youngest child accidentally knocked it over, breaking it into several pieces. I was so upset that my seven-year-old blurted out, "Mom, it's not your whole life, you know!"

I had overreacted, but what my daughter didn't know was that I didn't want to be in Alaska. I didn't know how I was going to cope. The shattered figurine reminded me that I was feeling broken inside.

In time, God did bind me up with encouragement from His Word—good friends, a writing opportunity, and spectacular outdoor adventures. For fourteen years and counting. No one can fix things like God.

—Carol

Lord God, only You can put my broken pieces back together.
Amen.

dream

Hope deferred makes the heart sick, but a dream fulfilled is
a tree of life.
—Proverbs 13:12 NLT

'm a nurse as well as a motivational speaker who encourages
women to pursue their God-given dreams. I call myself a
"dream midwife," so I find it exhilarating to talk to someone
who says she has no dream. A young woman attending a small
group in my home said precisely that! When I said everyone
has a dream, she insisted she didn't. I asked her what she
enjoyed. "I love to bake, but I am not a *real* baker."

"Maybe," I said, looking her in her eye, "baking is your
dream."

After a period of prayer and planning, she opened a
cake-baking business. She prays over every cake before she
starts, and her beautiful, tasty creations now grace many happy
occasions. All she needed was a little encouragement and help
pushing through.

—Penne

Lord, thank You for helping others give birth to their dreams.
Amen.

shine

Those who are wise will shine.
—Daniel 12:3 NIV

A military man, minister, postmaster, and raconteur, my father-in-law has been a great influence in my life. I was a teenager when I married his daughter, so he faced the task of fostering my journey into adulthood, a job that still isn't complete. One of the things he stressed early and often to me was the importance of always making sure one's dress shoes were properly shined. "A man's shoes reflect his character," he said. "If your shoes don't shine, people may assume you're lazy and careless."

I wear dress shoes infrequently nowadays, but I pray for my life to shine like a military man's shoes, ready for inspection. I crave a life lived out in wisdom that says to all around me that God is good, and even when troubles loom and confusion and darkness surround me, I still shine.

—Bob

Lord, make my life shine today. Amen.

sun

Keep your face to the sun and you will never
see the shadows.
—Helen Keller

T oby, my gray tabby cat, finds daily joy in pouncing on my
dog, Flash. He acts like a lion catching his prey. This makes
Flash, a small Jack Russell/Chihuahua mix, pretty anxious,
which is understandable. The only time they get along is when
they are napping in the sun. They bask in its warmth. All fierce-
ness and anxiety go away as the sun soothes body and spirit.

Like the sun, the warmth of Jesus's presence does the same
for me. When life feels wild, His faithful love leaves me feeling
sated and calm. In light of His mercy, anxiety and anger fade
away. There is no darkness in Jesus. His Holy Word is a lamp
for my feet, guiding my way. His face shines upon me, bringing
peace. Like the sun, Jesus brings light and life. I have all I need.
—Susanna

*Lord, even when I am in shadow, help me keep my face
to the Son. Amen.*

step

Be not afraid of growing slowly, be afraid
only of standing still.
—Chinese proverb

I tend to be an all-or-nothing kind of person. I don't like to do things halfway. But at times this approach is too big or too much for me to handle, so it leaves me feeling like a failure, like I'm less than.

Perhaps a better approach might be the "one-step-at-a-time" philosophy, to simply move forward, make headway, go in the right direction. I guess there's nothing wrong with this. After all, it means I'm not going backward!

I think God would be happy if I took one step at a time in pursuing a more fruitful faith life. If I embraced Him a bit more each day, if I acted on His behalf and in the way He asks, if I kept Him in sight as I move forward.

—Carolyn

God, thank You for being with me, whether I go backward or forward. Help me step in the right direction, closer to You. Amen.

beauty

A thing of beauty is a joy forever.
—John Keats

I call the New York Botanical Garden, in the Bronx, my "pretty gym." All year, even in the cold of winter, it's much more enjoyable to walk the three hilly miles of its main loop than spend half an hour on any aerobic machine. In spring and summer, the daffodils are sunny, the magnolias are fragrant, and the roses are worth going a few steps out of the way to see. But my favorite flowers are the peculiar plants. Last year I spotted a plant that bears a resemblance to a jellyfish. There's a spiky purple bloom that could be a disco ball from outer space. Orchids that look as if they just heard a great joke. All wonderful reminders that beauty takes many forms.

—Allison

Dear Lord, help me see the beauty in all of Your creations, especially those that seem a little odd upon first glance. Amen.

vision

If you want to move people, it has to be toward a vision
that's positive for them, that taps important values,
that gets them something they desire.
—Martin Luther King Jr.

I have a vision board that hangs on my bedroom wall. I see
it several times a day. It's covered with positive sayings and
magazine photos of long-held dreams dear to my heart.
Getting free of debt. Living close to our family. Owning a country home surrounded by trees. Publishing a book. In the fifteen
years since I created the vision board and tacked it up next to
my closet, most of my visions have come true (I'm on my sixth
book). Yes, I asked God to direct and help me. And He was
kind enough to say yes. Holding on to a vision—even when it
seemed impossible—made my faith soar.

—Jeanette

*Lord, please fill my heart and mind with Your positive visions
for my future and for this world. Amen.*

here

Be here, be now.
—Reynolds Price

I sat in my favorite chair, reading the morning's news. My wife entered, sat next to me, and started sharing about a work-related conundrum. I glanced up as she spoke, then back down at the news. "Are you here?" she asked. "Or somewhere else?" I confessed I hadn't been fully present before but was now giving her my full attention.

The patriarch Jacob had a dream of a stairway to heaven. On waking, he said, "Surely the LORD is in this place, and I did not know it" (Gen. 28:16 NKJV). As humans, we are either "here" or "there" (and sometimes "elsewhere"). But the Lord is always "here"; He is omnipresent, in every place. He is "Immanuel," meaning "God with us" (Matt. 1:23 NIV).

We can pray "here" simply to affirm His presence. Or to ask for His presence to be more evident to us.

—Bob

Lord, be here, be now. Amen.

there

For there the LORD bestows his blessing,
even life forevermore.
—Psalm 133:3 NIV

When our children were little, we played games together in the car. The alphabet game, of course. Perdiddle (finding cars with only one head lamp) and punch bug (lightly punching a fellow passenger's arm when a Volkswagen Beetle is spotted).

Every so often, I carry on the tradition these days, even when I'm alone in the car, with a prayer blessing game of sorts. I summarize the psalmist's words "It is as if the dew of Hermon were falling on Mount Zion. For there the LORD bestows his blessing, even life forevermore" (Ps. 133:3 NIV) into a one-word prayer: "There." I see someone sleeping on the sidewalk: "There, Lord." I pull over for an ambulance: "There." I drive by a church: "There." I pass a bunch of commuters waiting for a bus: "There."

—Bob

Father, bestow Your blessing here, there,
and everywhere today. Amen.

free

To forgive is to set a prisoner free and discover
that the prisoner was you.
—Lewis B. Smedes

Several years ago, my friend, Deborah, invited me to a women's encounter weekend. She said the retreat would change my life. I was curious yet guarded and decided to go and just "observe"—or so I thought. At one point during the retreat, the leader asked the group if there was anyone we needed to forgive. Two work colleagues came to mind. I knew I'd been harboring unforgiveness in my heart. Whenever the feelings surfaced, I tried dismissing them—but the heaviness remained. When the leader invited anyone to the altar who had a burden to unload, I stepped forward. As I forgave my coworkers, I was set free.

—Penne

Thank You, Lord, for showing me that as I free and release others, I, too, am freed. Amen.

wave

The most important thing for survival is communication
with someone, even if it's only a wave or a wink,
a tap on the wall.
—John McCain

O ne of the first movements babies employ is waving
their hands. These waves are random and meaning-
less at first, but it doesn't take long for little ones to
learn that when they wave, people wave back. It's an important
life lesson. Driving down a country road? Wave at other drivers
and they're sure to wave back. Spot a friend across a crowded
room? Waving might help her know you're there.

Waves are especially important during times of trouble,
when a car breaks down or, perhaps, in isolation during serious
illness. A wave, be it small and subtle or big and boisterous, lets
others know I'm there. That I see them. That I care. And just as
with babies, I'm almost certain to get a wave in return.

—Jennie

Remind us, God, that a wave is one more way to love. Amen.

brave

Watch, stand fast in the faith, be brave, be strong.
—1 Corinthians 16:13 NKJV

I f you looked up the definition of "strong" in the dictionary, my photo wouldn't be found beside it. Sometimes I get caught up in trying to do things perfectly. Other times, like Moses, I question my qualifications. Those thoughts set me up for fear and failure. Like the first time I met some ladies I'd lead in Bible study. *Would they like me? Could I guide them through the difficult passages, helping them apply God's Word to their lives?* Beneath the long table, my knees shook.

But just as God called Moses and equipped him well beyond his abilities, He'd called me to this task. I could be brave, trusting His wisdom, knowing He'd be there with me, as always. Once again, He strengthened my faith through overcoming my weaknesses. He even stopped my knees from trembling.

—Heidi

Lord, give me the strength to be brave when I feel unsure. Amen.

heal

I am the God of Abraham, the God of Isaac,
and the God of Jacob.
—Matthew 22:32 NIV

I have a friend named Cheryl who was miraculously healed of multiple sclerosis. She once was so weak that she had to be carried out of church; a few months later, after her healing, she was enviably strong and energetic. Another friend, Tim, was healed from cancer. And my friend Deb, after years of struggling, was healed emotionally from the effects of childhood sexual abuse.

I think of them often, as well as others I know who have been healed, when I pray for healing for myself or others. I'll remember how Jesus and Peter and others, referred to "the God of Abraham, Isaac, and Jacob," and I'll pray, "God of Cheryl, and Tim, and Deb, heal all who are hurting." Remembering God's healing power in their lives helps me to pray boldly, in faith.

—Bob

God of Abraham, Isaac, and Jacob, show Your healing
power today. Amen.

almost

This is the day which the Lord hath made.
—Psalm 118:24 KJV

I was in the checkout lane at my local Kroger when I overheard two middle-aged guys talking. "Don't you live in Morgantown?" one asked. "Almost did," the other said, shaking his head. "Almost went to the med school. Yeah, almost had me a nice little practice there."

Just then my eyes fell upon my day's to-do list. There were ten goals listed, but one seemed more than I could handle, so I'd crossed it out: Pick up a bouquet of daisies to take to Eva, my shut-in neighbor. That little voice I'd managed to shush earlier now spoke loud and clear. *Don't be an "almost," Roberta.*

I excused myself from the line and made a mad dash for the floral department. I had a sweet errand to run, and I'd almost missed the moment.

—Roberta

Lord, keep me from being an almost follower of You. Amen.

shelter

Whoever dwells in the shelter of the Most High will rest...
He will cover you with his feathers, and under
his wings you will find refuge.
—Psalm 91:1, 4 NIV

The last few years have been rough. Cancer, which was in remission for seventeen years, returned—twice. I'm happy to report that the cancer is gone, and I've been in remission for many months. Now I am a three-time winner!

Why am I telling you this? Because during those difficult years I realized that as important as physical shelter is, it was the shelter under the feathers of the Most High where I felt peaceful and not alone. I'd imagine myself as God's little bird, protected under His wing from the torrents of chemo and its battering side effects. As the storm of illness beat down on me, it would have to penetrate Him first. God became my true shelter.

—Michelle

Dear Lord, You are my shelter, my Protector, my Father, and You are always with me. Thank You. Amen.

oh

Oh, how my soul praises the Lord.
—Luke 1:46 NLT

Rain drizzled on us as we arrived at the Haleakala Crater
on the Hawaiian island of Maui. Clouds shrouded the
crater, limiting our view. My wife, chilled and disappointed,
returned to the tour bus, but I hoped to get at least a peek
at the site's natural beauty. With surprising suddenness, the
clouds lifted, revealing a stunningly colorful view of the crater.
Instinctively, my mouth opened wide. I exhaled an awed "Oh!"

The Magnificat is the famous prayer the teenaged Mary
prayed when an angel announced to her that she would be
the mother of Jesus, the Messiah. I love how the prayer above
begins in the New Living Translation.

Oh is a useful word in any season; it can be a syllable of
surprise, wonder, and praise. I make it a prayer when I see, hear,
or experience something extraordinary: "Oh!"

—Bob

*God, open my mouth wide with "ohs" of wonder
and praise today. Amen.*

frame

Through faith we understand that the worlds were
framed by the word of God.
—Hebrews 11:3 KJV

I tend to gravitate toward frames. Whenever I'm shopping,
I look for them. When I walk into someone's home, I move
toward them. For me, they hold important memories.

Just today, as I was cleaning, I had the chance to really look
at the frames I have around my house. My wedding photo,
photos of my boys throughout their lives, photos of my siblings
and parents. As I wiped off the frame holding a pen-and-ink
illustration of a saxophone player, I marvel at the gift God gave
my husband to be able to draw so beautifully.

Then I get to the windows—more frames! Every window is a
frame to the beauty of the world.

When I look at a frame—any frame—I see all that God
created.

—Carolyn

Hey, God, thanks for the memories! Amen.

shower

There shall be showers of blessing.
—D. W. Whittle

My wife and I recently moved across the country to Nevada, to live closer to our children and grand-children. It's our first time ever living in a desert. Yesterday, a beautiful spring day, set a new rainfall record for that date in our region: 0.2 inches (one-fifth of an inch). In such a climate, even a few drops of rain feel refreshing, and a shower prompts new growth to spring up everywhere.

That's what I crave for my life, and the lives of those around me. Like the words of Psalm 72:6 (NIV), attributed to King Solomon, "May he be like rain falling on a mown field, like showers watering the earth." I pray that word today, for my children and grandchildren: "Shower." For the neighbor who brought fresh-baked cookies to my door: "Shower." For the homeless woman pushing a shopping cart: "Shower." Over and over, heartfelt and hopeful: "Shower."

—Bob

Lord, shower me and those around me with blessings. Amen.

ready

Life is not a dress rehearsal.
—Rose Tremain, author

My dear dad was a stickler for time. One had to be ready! Especially when he was ready! As a child I worried. *What would happen if I were not ready?* One day I found out.

I was in the midst of a "costume" change. After all, changing into a different outfit at the last minute *is* part of most preteen girls' DNA. My dad, mother, and little sister were ready to go, but my older sister and I were not. Dad yelled, "Let's go!" a few times. Then it was quiet. When I heard something outside—was that the garage door opening?—I yelled to my sister, "They're in the car!"

We flew downstairs and ran outside waving our arms. Dad pulled the car back into the driveway, unlocked the doors, and we got in. His words to us that day still resonate: "Life is not a dress rehearsal. You have to be ready."

—Sue

Lord, help me to always be ready. Amen.

fall

Let my teaching fall like rain and my words descend
like dew, like showers on new grass, like abundant
rain on tender plants.
—Deuteronomy 32:2 NIV

This summer, my husband, Scott, and I walked to the park with our friends Ozzie and Melissa. Twenty minutes after arriving, Ozzie said, "Hey, guys, rain is headed our way." He was right. The blazing sun yielded to dark clouds. The rain began to fall in soft, fat droplets. Then in large, hard pellets. We were soaked when we got to the house. Every corner of the neighborhood was saturated. Droopy hydrangeas perked up. The lavender glistened. The thirsty lawns were revived.

Like my parched neighborhood, I need God's Spirit to fall on me, drenching me with refreshment and hope. His truth rains down guidance and blessing. Encouragement and wisdom are found when His words fall, refreshing my thirsty spirit.

—Susanna

*God, let Your words of wisdom and hope fall on my thirsty
soul and revive my spirit. Amen.*

simplicity

The ordinary acts we practice every day at home
are of more importance to the soul than their simplicity
might suggest.
—Thomas Moore

have a tendency to complicate things. I invite a few people for dinner for a simple reason: I want to spend time with those people. But if I don't keep a tight rein on myself, once the invitation is accepted, I'm off to the races, gradually adding complexity with each step. A more elaborate menu, fussing over my table décor, a sudden urge to have a perfectly clean house. I need to remember that freedom and beauty are found in simplicity. Sharing a simple meal with friends fills my heart and soul (and I hope, theirs).

—Julie

Heavenly Father, today and in the days ahead, help me to bring simplicity into my thoughts, words, and deeds. Amen.

honor

The best thing we can do is be a servant of God. It does good to stand up and serve others.
—Rev. Fred Shuttlesworth

Years ago, I was in a group touring major civil rights locations in the south. In Birmingham, Alabama, we learned that we'd meet the Rev. Fred Shuttlesworth, an iconic, veteran civil rights leader who was from Alabama. Shuttlesworth had been a close colleague of Rev. Dr. Martin Luther King Jr. and, like King, a courageous champion for justice dating back to the early 1950s. In fact, he made such an impact in that town that Birmingham–Shuttlesworth International Airport is named after him.

I was selected to introduce Rev. Shuttlesworth to our group. Beforehand, he had graciously shared a few highlights from his life that I could use in the introduction. His comments were riveting, compelling, and inspiring. What a tremendous joy it was to honor one of God's servants.

—Steve

Thank You, God, for the honor to serve others. Amen.

hallelujah

And every breath we drew was *Hallelujah*.
—Leonard Cohen, from the song "Hallelujah"

I was raised in a revivalist church that had been born in the Third Great Awakening. My childhood church services were punctuated with frequent shouts of "HALLELUJAH!" The most enthusiastic services sometimes ended with a "hallelujah windup," an indoor parade around the chapel while the participants sang and played musical instruments.

What I knew by training and exposure I learned later by linguistics: that *hallelujah* means "praise God," a Hebrew portmanteau (a mashup of two words), combining *hallel* (praise) and *Yah* (God). To this day, sometimes I'll get excited, even transported, in prayer, and the word gushes from me like a spring or waterfall: "Hallelujah." It enlivens my prayers, probably more than any other word. I pray it in good moods and bad, in ecstasy and misery, and it never fails to express my desires and lift my spirits. Hallelujah.

—Bob

*Hallelujah! For our Lord God Almighty reigns (Rev. 19:6 NIV).
Amen.*

fly

If birds can glide for long periods of time, then why can't I?
—Orville Wright

Upon returning home from the paradise known as Hawaii, I playfully told my husband, "I want to be a tour director when I grow up." Then I thought, *Why can't I? Other people do it. Why not me?* I pulled a sticky note from a pad and wrote: "WHY CAN'T I?" I stuck the note on the file cabinet where it remains today.

Over the next several months, I earned my tour director certification, pursued on-the-job training opportunities, and eventually secured a coveted job with an international tour operator. God provided ways for me to fly, both literally and figuratively. And that one simple question made up of three little words set it all in motion.

—Becky

God, wherever You lead, whatever You have planned for me, I'm ready to fly! Amen.

wind

Who has seen the wind? Neither you nor I but when the trees
bow down their heads, the wind is passing by.
—Christina Rossetti

I sit on the patio outside my home, enjoying the warm breeze
across my face. Watching the trees and flowers sway, I feel
the gentle wind on this day. What a difference from the times
during storms when the wind reveals another side—its awesome power, bending and breaking sturdy evergreens, ripping
roofs off buildings, and turning over cars like they were tiny
toys. I think God is much like that. He is as peaceful as a summer breeze, yet powerful like the formidable gusts of a hurri-
cane. The Almighty One reminds me of the ever-moving wind: I
can't see Him, but I know He's there.

—Barbranda

*Dear Lord, thank You for making Your presence known in gentle
breezes and powerful storms. Amen.*

wilderness

But Jesus often withdrew to the wilderness for prayer.
—Luke 5:16 NLT

It used to be difficult for me to understand why Jesus would go off alone into the wilderness to pray. Why didn't He go to a nice seashore? Or under a calming waterfall? Or why didn't He just pray in a comfortable guest room at a friend's house?

When I looked back at some of my wilderness moments—those dry places when I questioned whether God was even with me—it was in such times that I learned that it doesn't matter where I go to pray or live. Wherever I go, or whatever difficult situation I'm experiencing, God is there. He's faithful and present. In the wilderness God has made a way for me out of no way. In the wilderness God has healed my broken heart. In the wilderness I've enjoyed intimacy with God and learned how to wait on Him. The wilderness is the perfect place to pray.

—Penne

Lord, thank You for being with me in the wilderness.

imagine

Imagination is more important than knowledge. Knowledge
is limited. Imagination encircles the world.
—Albert Einstein

A minor shoulder injury causes me major pain and prevents me from weeding, so I can't do it anymore, but I've imagined new ways to garden. Now I plant petunias, coleus, and zinnias in huge, colorful pots. A flower bed that is overrun every spring with Goliath-sized crabgrass has been transformed (with the help of my weeding grand-daughter) into a maintenance-free rock garden adorned with large stones with the words *Hope* and *Grace* engraved on them. Finally, river rocks nestled between the stones complete my lovely, peaceful scene. Making it happen takes more time than I hope. But my God-given gift of imagination will not let me surrender. I keep working—because when I close my eyes, I can see the finished work of art.

—Jeanette

*God of All Creativity, light my imagination with
Your imagination. Amen.*

slow

Strange, what being forced to slow down
could do to a person.
—Nicholas Sparks, *The Last Song*

A friend of mine felt God was trying to get her attention, but she had a full schedule, so she just kept going and going, like the Energizer Bunny. Until the battery died, and she experienced an onset of Bell's palsy, a debilitating disease. Sidelined for a season, she told me that she finally slowed down enough to hear what God was saying.

I'm often reminded of my friend's experience, especially when I let external pressures dictate the pace of my life. When the only time I take a deep breath is when the doctor moves a cold stethoscope to a new position. At such times I pray one word: "Slow." It's a plea for God to slow me down, a reminder to "Be still before the LORD and wait patiently for him" (Ps. 37:7 NIV).

—Bob

Lord, slow me down that I may walk with You and not run ahead. Amen.

pencil

Keep my commands and you will live...write
them on the tablet of your heart.
—Proverbs 7:2–3 NIV

The first writing tool many children use is a sharp crayon. When they get the hang of that, most move on to a pencil. Why? Because it has an eraser, of course. A backward *S* can be fixed. Same with a *J* that hooks the wrong way. Arithmetic mistakes and misspelled words are no problem.

That's why, even as an adult, I've always loved a pencil. I can edit my grocery list. Erase and start over on Sudoku and crossword puzzles. Mess around with song lyrics I'm trying to write. But some writing needs to be done in ink. Checks and contracts. Birthday cards. Love letters. And, especially, eternal truths. Truths found in God's Holy Word. No erasers needed. Those I write on the tablet of my heart. In ink.

—Jennie

*Remind us, Heavenly Father, of the permanence of
Your commands. Amen.*

surround

The angel of the LORD encamps all around those
who fear Him, and delivers them.
—Psalm 34:7 NKJV

Recently my son and daughter-in-law took a long-awaited trip and left their two middle-school-aged children in my care for a week. Miles and Mia were enrolled in a new school, and each of them had described to me some daunting challenges they were facing. So, each morning I prayed as I dropped them off at school, as I watched them enter, and as I drove back home. Over and over I prayed a single word: "Surround."

That single word expressed so much, more than I could otherwise express. Surround them with Your angels. Surround them with Your care and protection. Surround them with good friends, good influences, good teachers and coaches. Surround them with wisdom and understanding, foresight and insight, encouragement and blessing. Surround.

—Bob

Lord, surround me and mine this day and every day. Amen.

life

Why, you do not even know what will happen tomorrow. What is your life? You are a mist that appears for a little while and then vanishes.

—James 4:14 NIV

L ife is so fragile," my husband often says, especially upon hearing the news of a tragic fatal accident or the sudden, unexpected passing of a family member or friend. As a child, it seemed as if life would go on forever, and the reason for living was to have fun. As a young adult, I felt I was indestructible and life was a breeze. As I grow into my senior years, I can see how life passes by in the blink of an eye. It truly is like a mist that vanishes. Now I think more about the legacy and imprint I will leave on this earth. In the meantime, I thank the Lord for my life every day. It truly is a gift from God.

—Barbranda

Lord, help me to treasure the life You've given me. Amen.

chosen

But at the heart of the gospel is this truth, we are called and chosen by God to join in with the dance of the trinity, Father, Son and Holy Spirit.
—Tim Hughes

I enjoy remembering the evening my husband and I watched our local orchestra perform. The conductor explained their next piece was unique, composed in such a way to allow each type of instrument to sound as if it had a solo. These players had been chosen with care by the conductor. They understood the beauty of the "dance." Listening, I sat in awe, hearing a crowd of musicians play together, yet every person's part was significant.

Like that symphony, my part in this dance of faith is small, but important. Without me, God's song would be incomplete. He chose me specifically for the part I play, and I'm honored.
—Heidi

Lord, thank You for choosing me to be in Your family. Amen.

link

All of our ancestors give us the precious gift of life.
—Laurence Overmire

I take after my dad's side of the family and his Czech heritage, from sharing a similar look to enjoying traditional food. My dad's parents died when I was young, so I didn't know them, but I spent a lot of time with my dad's sisters.

Aunt Ethel was a single woman all her life, independent and generous with her love and pocketbook. Aunt Olga tended a huge garden and was proud to share her harvest with us. Aunt Elinore, whom I always called the fun one—because she loved to laugh—would invite me to sleep over. She would make one of my favorite Czech dinners and we would hang out. I felt special and loved by each of these women.

My dad's sisters have been gone for many years, but I will forever cherish the link I have to them and my heritage.

—Carolyn

Thank you, God, for the love of extended family. Amen.

attitude

A cheerful heart is good medicine.
—Proverbs 17:22 NIV

An elderly gentleman in my doctor's office waiting room pointed to the hand I'd bruised trying to move a table. "Honey!" he said loudly. "Do you have *leukemia*?" As his words garnered attention from the other patients, I felt my cheeks redden in embarrassment and my spirit grumble. Then it hit me. This was a chance to tell the whole crowd about my miracle. "No," I answered so everyone could hear. "For fifty-five years I lived in terrible pain. But two years ago, I heard from heaven, and now I don't even have to take a Tylenol." I patted my bruise and smiled: "Every morning, I still have to pinch myself to believe it's real." Soon the whole room was praising Jesus, the best medicine of all.

—Roberta

Help me to change today's attitude, Lord, with Your attitude.
Amen.

zeal

The zeal of the LORD of armies will accomplish this.
—Isaiah 9:7 NASB

There are many synonyms for zeal—passion, intensity, hustle, determination. They all sound intimidating and exhausting. But God does not get tired. His zeal is both active and restful. This passage in Isaiah refers to God the Father sending His Son Jesus into the world with the promise there will be no end to His kingdom of peace and righteousness. A promise made seven hundred years before the birth of Christ! God kept the faith with His intention. He waited for the right time. His determination to give the world a Savior never dimmed. His zeal inspires me to not give up. To keep steady. Keep hopeful. God's zeal flows from His heart—inviting me along for the ride. Inviting me to trust Him.

—Carol

What will Your zeal accomplish in my life, Lord? I'm excited!
Amen.

refine

Blot out, correct, insert, refine. Enlarge, diminish, interline.
—Jonathan Swift

'm a writer and editor, constantly in the process of refining sentences. Almost every sentence, once created, can be improved. Verbs can be strengthened, repetition eliminated, structure changed. Happily, sentences never object or complain, though some can seem resistant, even obstinate.

I want to be the kind of person who is constantly being refined by my Heavenly Father. I want to welcome His "edits" of my life and character without objection or complaint—even when the refining process feels painful. I know that "the words of the LORD are flawless, like silver purified in a crucible, like gold refined seven times" (Ps. 12:5–6 NIV). The changes He makes in my life are wise; they're meant to prosper me, not harm me (see Jer. 29:11), that I may live to the praise of His glorious grace (see Eph. 1:6).

—Bob

Lord of my life: Blot out, correct, insert, refine, enlarge, diminish, as You will. Amen.

comma

Practice the pause. When in doubt, pause. When angry,
pause. When tired, pause. When stressed, pause.
And when you pause, pray.
—TobyMac

had a friend in college who randomly inserted commas
throughout her compositions. I asked her once why she
generously used that punctuation mark. She said she wasn't
really sure how to use it, so she put one wherever she thought
it was needed. I explained that commas are mostly meant
to indicate a pause, a natural breath, a moment to breathe.
It's sort of like what God does for me. He inserts a comma in
various spots in my life because He wants me to stop and rest
or learn a lesson. Sometimes I recognize it as such; other times
I think I'm facing a defeat or the end. But it's only the Lord's
comma—a pause, not a period.

—Barbranda

*Lord, thank You for the pauses in my life. May I use them
to draw closer to You. Amen.*

ponder

Whatever is true, whatever is noble, whatever is right, whatever
is pure, whatever is lovely, whatever is admirable—if anything
is excellent or praiseworthy—think about such things.
—Philippians 4:8 NIV

Drowsiness overtakes me in the late evening, stretched
out in my recliner, snuggled under a blanket, mindlessly
watching TV. I force myself to get up, put on my paja-
mas, and go to bed. But the instant my head reaches the pillow, my eyes pop open and the drowsiness disappears. That's
when the pondering begins. I review my day and camp out on
encounters that discourage me. Then I worry about each family
member equally and by name. If I'm still awake, I move on to
a troubled world, the future, and concerns of that sort. Should
I be surprised when my own petrifying scream wakes me from
a nightmare a few hours later? I need to focus my thoughts on
things that are lovely and praiseworthy.

—Becky

God, remind me to ponder positive things. Amen.

focus

When walking, walk. When eating, eat.
—Zen proverb

As the mother of three children born in rapid succession, I had to multitask to survive. I cooked supper while helping with homework. Folded laundry while telling a bedtime story. Bandaged scraped knees while shooing the cat out the door.

Those children are grown and on their own now. Semi-retired and living alone, I try to resist the urge to multitask. I find it easier to focus on what's important if I do only one thing at a time. But old habits are hard to break. Time after time, I have to yank myself off the busy hamster wheel and concentrate on the task at hand. Unloading the dishwasher while not listening to the news. Watering the garden while not talking on the phone. Eating breakfast while not reading anything, including the back of the cereal box.

Most of all, praying with my focus completely on God.

—Jennie

Lord, help me to do just one thing at a time. Amen.

breakthrough

When you are tempted to give up, your breakthrough is
probably just around the corner.
—Joyce Meyer

Florence couldn't understand my words, and I couldn't understand hers. As activities director of a nursing home, I had stopped by her room to welcome our new patient. She was alone. Frightened. In a country foreign to her. When I offered a handshake, she grabbed my hand with both of hers and squeezed. After that, I visited Florence often, and each time she seemed a bit sadder. I desperately wanted to encourage her, but the language barrier limited my ideas. Then a nurse mentioned that Florence spoke French. I went home and searched for my old college French book. The next day I entered her room and said, "*Bonjour! Comment allez-vous?*" She lit up like the Eiffel Tower and rattled off a response that I couldn't translate. It was a small breakthrough but, oh, what a joyous one.

—Becky

God, help me hang on and trust You for a breakthrough. Amen.

morning

Morning is the best time to thank God.
—Analiza Garcia

---

start every morning with a cup of coffee and my list. *How quickly can I get to those things and cross them off,* I wonder?
Many times, because I'm caught up in my list, the beauty of the moment passes me by. Instead of focusing on the tasks in front of me, today I take a few minutes to see the sunlight shifting a path across my living room floor. Even with the windows closed, I hear the birds chirping, a sure sign of spring. The branches of a flowering crabapple sway in the gentle breeze. I nuzzle my eight-year-old Lab instead of shooing him away. Framed photos are everywhere, and I smile as I remember when each was taken.

Each morning is an awakening of a new day and the beauty God has surrounded me with. I am grateful.

—Carolyn

Dear God, help me to stop each morning and really see all of my blessings. Amen.

sabbath

For He has spoken in a certain place of the
seventh day in this way: "And God rested on the
seventh day from all His works."
—Hebrews 4:4 NKJV

I was tired. The last few weeks had been exhausting, but my groggy body managed to get up and push through my daily three-mile walk. As I walked, the host of the podcast I was listening to asked the guest to share some final words of wisdom with the audience. "Always have a Sabbath rest each week. Turn off your phone and watch a funny movie to rest your soul." As I listened, those words resonated within me. Sabbath rest was what my weary mind, body, and soul needed, and I embraced that idea like it was gold. If God needed to rest from His work, then maybe I need to rest from my work too.

—Penne

Dear Father, help me to take and enjoy regular Sabbath rest.
Amen.

chesed

Show Your marvelous lovingkindness.
—Psalm 17:7 NKJV

I gave a series of talks to a group of pastors in Germany, using a translator. Before each talk, the translator (who became a friend) would check with me on some of the finer points of translation. Some words, he said, just don't translate well from one language to another, so he wanted to make sure the word he planned to use would convey my intended meaning.

Chesed is a Hebrew word from the Bible that is so rich that no English word captures its full meaning. English Bibles usually translate it as "lovingkindness," "mercy," and "steadfast love," but *chesed* encompasses all of those meanings—and more. I often use the original word when I pray. A family friend is hospitalized and in serious condition; a relative is suffering work burnout; a neighbor is facing financial hardship. I pray *chesed* for them all.

—Bob

Lord, show Your marvelous lovingkindness in and through me today. Amen.

music

He will rejoice over thee with joy; he will rest in his love,
he will joy over thee with singing.
—Zephaniah 3:17 KJV

Working in a busy pediatric emergency department is a special place to be. I get to share in some of the most sacred moments of a family's life. There are moments of pain and sorrow, but also joy, gratitude and miracles.

I was caring for a sickle-cell patient who would come in frequently with excruciating pain. One day as this precious little girl writhed in discomfort, she heard me humming and immediately asked me to sing to her. My singing seemed to distract my little patient, the music providing healing of some sort. As a nurse, my typical approach to pain management is medicine, but on this particular day I saw God use music to soothe anxiety and pain.

—Penne

Dear God, thank You for rejoicing and singing music over me. Amen.

laugh

Laugh and the world laughs with you.
—Ella Wheeler Wilcox

There's really nothing like laughter to make even your worst day a little brighter. There's a certain sensibility required to bring on a giggle. It means not taking life so seriously and trusting God. It's about letting go.

I remember a night when I tried in vain to make my young daughter behave at the dinner table, an ongoing battle that felt all important. My blood pressure was surging—when she stood in her chair and began shimmying her tiny hips. "Watch this," she said, bursting out in song. I laughed uncontrollably. So did my wife and son. And in that moment, I felt God's love wash over me. Fourteen years later, that evening, when it seemed I'd never be able to teach my daughter discipline, remains one of my fondest memories.

—Evan

Lord, I'm so grateful You have a sense of humor and gave me one too. Amen.

glorious

Now, our God, we give you thanks, and praise
your glorious name.
—1 Chronicles 29:13 NIV

I have a perfect sunset view from the back of our home in
Idaho. There is a wide field behind our lot that ends on a high
ridge, framing the dusky sky. As the sun sets with a vibrant
glow, it casts off glorious rays of hot pink, brilliant yellow,
and fiery orange. I can't capture the sky's glory with words or
pictures. Neither do it justice. But I try anyway, saying, "It's
amazing!" or "Stunning!"

I have a similar feeling when I try to express the glory of
God. Words are too small to describe who He is and what
He does. I am stunned by His mercy. I am gobsmacked by
His unconditional love. I am awed by His faithfulness. In His
glorious presence, all I can do is thank Him.

—Susanna

*Thank You, Lord, for Your glorious love and wonderful provision.
You amaze me. Amen.*

increase

And Jesus increased in wisdom and stature,
and in favor with God and men.
—Luke 2:52 NKJV

Too many times I've heard myself say, "I'm not a patient person," or "I have one nerve left and you're getting on it!" I blamed such outbursts on either the amount of caffeine I drank that morning or my Irish ancestry. Until the sweet voice of Jesus pulled me up short. In the secret place of my heart, where I try to hide my faults, He whispered, "Jeanette, you have all the fruit of the Spirit you need, including patience (see Gal. 5:22–23). You just need to exercise it and it will increase." Oh, so that's how it works. I no longer get to play the blame game, or use the Irish genes rationalization? In that case, Lord, I need Your supernatural help!

—Jeanette

Thank You, God, for giving me all the love and power I need to increase my patience. Help me depend on You and less on myself. Amen.

again

LORD, I have heard of your fame; I stand in awe of your deeds, LORD. Repeat them in our day.
—Habakkuk 3:2 NIV

I sat with my wife, children, and grandchildren in our living room when the youngest grandchild (at that time) approached. My legs were crossed, and he straddled my lower leg as if riding a horse. I bounced him up and down several times, to his delight. Then I stopped. "Do it again!" he commanded, and I complied. "Again!" And "Again!" His enjoyment far outlasted my strength. I eventually had to beg for permission to rest my weary leg, or he may have ridden his imaginary "horsey" all day.

Our Heavenly Father needs no such respite. I often beg Him to repeat His mercies and miracles of previous days. "Do it again!" I pray. Sometimes it's just the single word "Again!" And "Again!" And He does. His mercies—and miracles—are new every morning.

—Bob

I've seen You do marvelous things, Lord. Do them again. And again. Amen.

enjoy

So I saw there is nothing better for a person than
to enjoy their work.
—Ecclesiastes 3:22 NIV

I was mixing up a big bowl of pimento cheese when my neighbor Lucy tapped on my back door and let herself in. When she saw what I was doing, her eyes grew wide. "You know you can buy ready-made pimento cheese at the store," she said with a smile. I nodded and kept scraping the block of extra-sharp cheddar along the blades of the metal grater. "Or you can buy cheese that's already shredded," she added. "You don't have to work so hard."

I dumped a jar of pimentos onto the pile of cheese and added two generous spoonsful of mayonnaise. "It's not really work if it's something I enjoy," I told her. I stirred the ingredients together, spread a dollop on a saltine cracker, and handed it to her. "Enjoy!" I said. "It's homemade."

—Jennie

Heavenly Father, teach us to enjoy the tasks set before us. Amen.

time

Yesterday is gone. Tomorrow has not yet come.
We have only today. Let us begin.
—Mother Teresa

What time is it?" my mother asked for the third time in five minutes. Mom has Alzheimer's disease and she soon forgets whatever someone tells her. She is losing her grasp of time and constantly asks my age. Whenever I answer her questions, she'll say, "It can't be that late" or "You can't be that old." Although the repetitive nature of our conversations can be a little tiresome, I try to live in the moment and take in Mom's expressions, appearance, and the sound of her voice. I know that we both have more time behind us than ahead of us. The Lord is telling me to make the most of the minutes, hours, and days. Tomorrow is not promised.

—Barbranda

Lord, make me mindful of how I spend my time and help me live in the moments You're giving me. Amen.

keep

A time to keep and a time to throw away.
—Ecclesiastes 3:6 NIV

The stuff had taken over—tools, outdated files, books, clothing, record albums, and a collection of old clocks and radios that my husband had declared "antiques." It was all packed tight in our basement, jumbled together in no apparent order. Every time I went downstairs, I felt overwhelmed and frustrated. Finally, help came with a push from our son during one of his visits. Over several days, we sorted through the piles and decided what to keep, discard, or give away. We toted countless bags of clothing to Goodwill, gave away boxes of books, and shredded tons of documents. And we started to organize the things we kept. The house felt lighter with less clutter, items neatly stacked away. Organizing is a journey, but at least we took the first step—and perhaps blessed others with the giveaways.

—Barbranda

Lord, help me to know what to keep and what to let go. Amen.

come

LORD, do not be far from me. You are my strength; come
quickly to help me.
—Psalm 22:19 NIV

Texting has introduced a new brevity into some of my
conversations. Recently a friend texted to ask if I still
needed his help with an outdoor project I had mentioned to him earlier. I sent a one-word reply: "Come."

A frequent phrase on the lips—and pens—of the Bible's
songwriters was "come quickly, LORD, to help me" (Ps. 40:13
NIV). Not that God is ever far, but we often need reminders
that He's present with us. "Come" reminds us of our need, of
His willing presence, of His available strength and help. Taking
a moment to utter the single word—"Come"—invites the Lord
into my chaos and stress and brings the Prince of Peace into my
situation. Into my mind. Into the moment. So, when necessary, I
take a breath, close my eyes, and say: "Come."

—Bob

Lord, I pray: Come. Come now. Come quickly. Come often. Amen.

humor

Laughter without a tinge of philosophy is but a sneeze of humor. Genuine humor is replete with wisdom.
—Mark Twain

One of my favorite things about my nephew Alex is that he got my sister's sense of humor. Christine and I don't always see eye to eye. She's a morning lark, I'm a night owl. She works in science, I work with words. But I've always been able to depend on her to make me laugh so hard my stomach hurts. I remember her saying once on a road trip, "I'm in a car, I'm bored—I'm cardboard!" Alex tells elaborate, outlandish stories and can be pretty silly. I take it as a big compliment when I make either Christine or Alex laugh.

—Allison

God, thank You for the joys of humor and laughter. They bring people of different generations and personalities together to smile. Amen.

favorite

"For I know the plans I have for you," declares the Lord,
"...plans to give you hope and a future."
—Jeremiah 29:11 NIV

A
fter my parents passed away, my brother's wife, Ellen, was determined to keep our family together with future traditions. My birthday party was her first effort. No detail was spared. Ellen went from store to store to find every ingredient to make the fresh fruit salad I adore. The whole affair was so personal, it felt like I was her favorite. I hoped no one else noticed. Then one of my sisters had a birthday, and Ellen planned the extravaganza around Rebekkah's favorite color yellow. Everything from the flowers to the cake to her presents was in that sunny hue. As we drove away from the party, Rebekkah said, "If I didn't know better, Roberta, I'd swear I was Ellen's favorite."

—Roberta

Thank You for people, Lord, who treat everyone sublimely the same. Surely I'd be in a fix if You played favorites! Amen.

light

For you were once darkness, but now you are light in the
Lord. Live as children of light.
—Ephesians 5:8 NIV

I entered the dark house through an unlocked door. My
friend hadn't answered the phone for hours. At two in the
afternoon, all the curtains were closed, and no lights were
on. When I called her name, she didn't answer. I roamed from
room to room until I found her, sleeping in a bedroom. She
awoke, startled, and explained that she was feeling a bit blue
because somebody had hurt her feelings. I said, "Well, get up,
and get dressed. It's a beautiful day outside!" She slipped on
some clothes while I opened every curtain in the house. Then
we stepped into the sunshine, and my friend's blue afternoon
became a bright one. Maybe that's what Jesus wants me to
do—throw open the curtains for others, allowing His light to
illuminate the darkness around them.

—Becky

Jesus, show me someone who needs a little light today. Amen.

remove

I will give you a new heart and put a new spirit in you;
I will remove from you your heart of stone and give
you a heart of flesh.
—Ezekiel 36:26 NIV

One spring, my preteen daughter and I wanted to plant a vegetable garden. We mapped it out in our yard and started work. Soon we hit an obstacle: a large, heavy rock. We could've planted around it or moved the location of the garden, but we eventually removed the rock. That summer we enjoyed the fruits—and vegetables—of our labor… especially zucchini. Lots of zucchini.

It can be as hard—harder, even—to remove from my life the things that trip me up and tear me down. Some are external; many originate in me. Some are easy to remove; others are excavated only with great difficulty, even pain. So, I pray: "Remove." Remove it all. Remove it completely.

—Bob

Lord, remove everything in my life that trips me up or tears
me down. Amen.

open

An open heart is an open mind.
—Dalai Lama

M any years ago, I heard a speaker at a business conference say that if you keep your mouth open a little when you're not speaking, you'll seem more "open." I guess keeping your lips pressed together can transmit an appearance of disapproval or inflexibility.

I want to be open, yet I sometimes find it hard to be, especially when what comes next usually involves change. But being open also provides me with an opportunity to reflect—on myself, my relationships, my behavior. And being open provides me with an opportunity to see the beauty all around me, feel love and joy deep in my heart, and share my life with those who matter most to me.

Actually, being open provides me with a lot of opportunities. Period.

—Carolyn

Help me to always be open to the life You have created for me, Lord, so that I'm not afraid to be open to all the possibilities that await. Amen.

solitude

The happiest of all lives is a busy solitude.
—Voltaire

I love people and parties and conversations, so people are often surprised when I say I lean toward introvert on personality tests. But when the question asks, "When and where am I most renewed?" I answer: when I am alone. My most rewarding times are spent beneath the cherry tree on my small glider bench. But they could also be beside a still lake or walking quietly along our mountain road. The secret is I am not truly alone. My thoughts are constantly connecting with Jesus—sharing my life, giving thanks, asking questions, listening for His voice, meditating on His Word. I have discovered solitude grows a rich inner life that has become my best friend.

—Carol

Jesus, You showed a love for people and a love for solitude.
Help me neglect neither. Amen.

help

This is a hard planet, and we're a vulnerable species.
And all I can do is pray: Help.
—Anne Lamott, in *Help, Thanks, Wow*

O ne winter when we were kids, my brother and I were playing in the woods near our home in Ohio. The pond was frozen, and I ventured out onto the surface. A crack started beneath my feet, and the ice gave way. I caught myself before falling completely into the frigid water, but I couldn't climb out. I hung on, desperate. "Help?" I squeaked. My brother ran toward me and inched out on the ice, extending a sturdy branch. I gripped it and he slowly pulled me to solid ground.

"Help." It's perhaps the most instinctive prayer we ever pray. Whether shouted or squeaked, a plea for rescue or simple support, whether our need is sudden or sustained, the God of the universe is "our help and our shield" (Ps. 33:20 NIV). "Help" brings Him to our aid.

—Bob

O God, make haste to help me. Amen.

celebrate

"This is a day you are to commemorate; for the generations to come you shall celebrate it as a festival to the Lord."
—Exodus 12:14 NIV

God must love a party, because the Old Testament is full of festivals and celebrations that He commanded the children of Israel to hold every year. (The word *celebrate* appears sixty-eight times in the Scriptures.) Some of these celebrations last an entire week. All commemorate events that God wanted people always to remember, like their deliverance from Egypt. These festivities are meant to strengthen their faith, and to this day, Jews celebrate them.

I must admit that when I celebrate, it's usually somebody's birthday or a new baby or a job promotion—all worth celebrating! But maybe I can celebrate God's abundance in my life in a way that would strengthen my journey of faith.

I think I'll have a *Thank You, God* party. Want to come?

—Michelle

Thank You, God, for the many ways we can celebrate You.

story

Storytelling reveals meaning without committing
the error of defining it.
—Hannah Arendt

When I worked in a children's bookstore, a large part of my job was finding a book someone was looking for based on a few precious, sometimes distorted, details of a story. People were always coming to me with hazy memories of their "book." That is, the story someone enjoyed hearing over and over as a child. When I found the right book, there was nothing better than holding it up and seeing that flash of recognition as a face flooded with joy. "That's it!" she'd say, before turning it over in her hands and plopping down to read it right there on the bookstore's storytelling pillows. How could something you barely remember be a part of you? That's the magic of a good story.

—Meg

Heavenly Father, thank You for the infinite number of stories You've given us and the wisdom You've hidden in all of them.
Amen.

courageous

Have I not commanded you? Be strong and courageous.
Do not be afraid; do not be discouraged, for the LORD your
God will be with you wherever you go.
—Joshua 1:9 NIV

I scanned the room as the nurse and anesthesiologist prepped me for an operation. I'd fought cancer years earlier, and this surgery would reduce the chances of it recurring. As the moment for me to be rolled into the operating room loomed closer, I closed my eyes. Why wasn't I nervous?

The nurse took my hand and offered to pray with me. Her words spread calm over any doubts I may have felt. I knew I'd be fine. Because even before her precious prayer, I'd sensed the presence of the Lord. I knew He'd be with me the entire time, guiding the hands of the medical staff, clarifying thoughts, and most of all, holding me close. I would be strong and courageous. How could I be otherwise with Him at my side?

—Heidi

Lord, knowing You are always with me keeps me strong and courageous. Thank You. Amen.

shalom

The LORD gives strength to his people; the LORD blesses his
people with peace.
—Psalm 29:11 NIV

O n my first trip to Israel, I was delighted to be greeted,
repeatedly, with "Shalom." The airport customs agent
stamps my passport and hands it back to me, saying,
"Shalom." I approach the hotel desk clerk, who smiles and
says, "Shalom." I enter a restaurant, and the maître d' greets
me with "Shalom." I learned quickly, answering my hotel wake-up
call, "Shalom."

Shalom means "peace" in Hebrew, but in Israel it's used to
say "hello" and "goodbye" too. The word is used in the Bible not
only for "peace" but also to mean a state of wholeness, flourishing, and happiness. Knowing this, I like to pray the word *shalom*
for my family and friends. I scroll through my prayer list, whisper-
ing "shalom" for each person and every need, asking God to
bless them all with peace, wholeness, flourishing, and happiness.

—Bob

Lord, bless me and those around me today with shalom. Amen.

shift

And the LORD spoke to me, saying: "You have skirted
this mountain long enough; turn northward."
—Deuteronomy 2:2–3 NKJV

Aching back, aching shoulders, aching knees, aching
feet. You name it—it ached. My husband's body dis-
played the consequences of lifting cases of soft drinks
for fifteen years. He considered seeking a new job, yet the
promise of a less strenuous supervisor position kept him moving the bubbly products from truck to store shelf. Ten years
have passed, and he is still lifting and still in pain, only worse.
Had my husband made a life shift back then, today would have
looked much different. But it's not too late. God and I have
encouraged him to shift now toward a healthier and happier
future. He has circled the mountain long enough.

—Becky

God, do I need a directional shift in any area of my life?
Show me the way. Amen.

favor

Surely, Lord, you bless the righteous; you surround them with
your favor as with a shield.
—Psalm 5:12 NIV

We took our nine-year-old daughter and a friend to one of those medieval restaurant-and-show establishments where knights in armor ride horses and joust one another for the pleasure of the diners. One of the knights, before a joust, trotted his horse our way, pointed to our daughter, and tossed a red rose to her. She was delighted, of course. For the remainder of the evening, she rooted and cheered for that knight against all others.

An image like that animates the one-word prayer "Favor" for me. I already live in God's favor. I am a recipient of His grace. Even so, I beg for Him to single me out and toss me a rose, so to speak. When applying for a job: "Favor." Before an important meeting: "Favor." Upon entering the dentist's office: "Favor."

—Bob

*Remember me, Lord, when You show favor to
Your people (Ps. 106:4 NIV). Amen.*

mission

My mission in life is not merely to survive, but to thrive;
and to do so with some passion, some compassion,
some humor, and some style.
—Maya Angelou

Back in high school, I thought my mission in life was going to be telling people what to wear. One of my grandmas was a clothing buyer and had great style. That led me to journalism school so I could write for fashion magazines. Life, of course, had other plans. In the army I produced newsletters to keep my fellow soldiers and their families informed. An internship in graduate school saw me writing about math and science for kids. Now I write about people who make their communities better. It's so rewarding that I can't imagine my mission being anything else.

—Allison

Lord, I will always be thankful You led me down the path of using writing to help others. I didn't know it was my mission, but You did. Amen.

wonder

You are the God who does wonders; You have declared
Your strength among the peoples.
—Psalm 77:14 NKJV

I haven't seen any seas part so an entire nation can walk
through on dry ground. Or witnessed water change to costly
wine. Or watched as a man born lame receive God's power to
dance and leap. All those miracles are recorded in the Bible.

But the little miracles I behold every day assure me of a
God of love and wonders. Fireflies that blink and wink the
summer nights away. Hummingbirds that buzz inches from
my face on their way to a crimson flower. Chipmunks scurry-
ing down a tree. Roses that willingly share their spicy, sweet
perfume. Orioles, bluebirds, and finches in a panorama of color
at the bird feeders hanging from our eaves. Mother Nature
smiling? Or the Creator showing His dear children how much
He loves them?

—Jeanette

*Lord, You are creativity personified. Thank You for amazing us
with Your many wonders. Amen.*

comfort

This is my wish for you: Comfort on difficult days.
—Ralph Waldo Emerson

My mother died when I was fourteen years old. To this day, the fragrance of roses or a Nat King Cole standard can revive in me a potent mixture of love and sorrow. And to this day, I feel a strong affinity and empathy for children and young people who lose a parent.

That's how comfort works. The Bible says that God "comforts us in all our troubles, so that we can comfort those in any trouble with the comfort we ourselves receive from God" (2 Cor. 1:3–4 NIV). God often redeems our sufferings by equipping us and giving us opportunities to extend comfort to others. Sometimes we do that in person by sitting or crying with a struggling or heartbroken friend, but always we can pray for God's comfort to visit them, even with a one-word prayer I pray often: "Comfort."

—Bob

God of all comfort, comfort all who are suffering today. Amen.

hum

There's no better way to calm your mind and boost
your spirits than by humming a happy tune.
—*Psychology Today*

E arly in life, I realized I didn't have a strong singing voice. In
fact, I had a terrible singing voice. I thought I had no talent
for musical instruments, either, until I discovered the kazoo.
All you had to do was hum and—voilà!—there was music.

Though I rarely play the kazoo, I've never stopped humming.
Sometimes I don't even realize I'm doing it. Preparing a community meal in the church kitchen one Thanksgiving, I felt a friend's
hand on my shoulder. "I love that you're humming," she said.

"I was?"

"You sure were," she told me. "It sounded like 'We Gather
Together.' Please don't stop!"

I didn't. And I won't. Humming is one little way I can lift my
spirits and the spirits of those around me. And I don't even
need a kazoo!

—Jennie

I praise You with music, Lord, however humble it might be.
Amen.

kindness

A single act of kindness throws out roots in all directions, and the roots spring up and make new trees.
—Amelia Earhart

I used to think that tumbleweeds were dead plants that rolled across the desert, forlorn and hopeless. Not so. When a dead tumbleweed tumbles along, it flings thousands of seeds far and wide, leaving a trail of seedlings everywhere they go. I know this because I have pulled up thousands of tiny tumbleweeds from my yard. There is an endless supply.

I have decided to model myself after the tumbleweed when it comes to spreading kindness. Encircled by God's grace and mercy, I have the ability to unleash His goodness upon those around me. In tumbleweed fashion, I want to fling an endless supply of kindness toward the people I meet each day, leaving a trail of hope and peace everywhere I go.

—Susanna

God, unleash Your kindness in and through me. Amen.

exercise

You have to exercise, or at some point you'll just break down.
—Barack Obama

Sheryl kept nudging me for weeks to join her for a walk in our neighborhood. I kept coming up with reasons why I couldn't—deadlines to meet, appointments to go to, dinner to prepare. Truth is, I don't like to exercise. Never have, although I know it's good for me. Finally, one morning I rolled out of bed determined to get up and get moving. I called Sheryl and we met to do a two-mile walk around a nearby lake on a humid and sunny summer day. We started off at a good clip, chatting nonstop and cheerfully greeting other walkers we passed along the way. By the end, I was sweaty and energized. That wasn't so bad. I just had to make up my mind to take the first step.

—Barbranda

Lord, help me to take better care of myself so that I'll be around to serve You and others. Amen.

now

Now is the right time to listen, the day to be helped.
—2 Corinthians 6:2 MSG

Most of us spend a lot of time replaying the past or thinking about the future. Both can be stressful. Each removes us from the present and cheats us of the full blessing of this life, this day, this moment—this "now."

The single, simple word *now* can be a way of awakening yourself to the beauty of your own life, a way of fully breathing in and breathing out the blessing of being alive...now. Or, when things are happening fast and the need for God's intervention is urgent, a sharp, single word—"now"—can say it all.

Whatever the past has been, whatever the future may hold, praying "now" can be a helpful way to focus and calm your mind and heart, or call into action the help you need, right here, right now.

—Bob

Lord, thank You for "now." Help me to live it. Amen.

reveal

Whenever I'm confused about something, I ask God to reveal the answers to my questions, and he does.
—Beyoncé Knowles

I've worn glasses since my early thirties. For many years, I would put off going to the optometrist for a new examination, not wanting to spend the money. But when I put on my new prescription, I was amazed; everything was so much clearer and sharper.

I do something similar on a spiritual level—like the servant of the prophet Elisha, who when he awoke one morning saw himself surrounded by a hostile army. But Elisha prayed, "Open his eyes, Lord, so that he may see" (2 Kings 6:17 NIV), and the servant suddenly saw not only that God was in control but also that He was about to lead Elisha and his servant to victory. Sometimes I pray the word "Reveal" (often repeatedly) to ask God to let me see beyond the obvious to the providential, even the miraculous.

—Bob

Open my eyes, Lord, and reveal Your glory. Amen.

goodbye

The most difficult thing for most people to say in twenty-five words or less is "goodbye."
—Author unknown

You'd think that saying goodbye to difficulty would be a breeze. I recently discovered that changing how I view myself can be a challenge, regardless of the circumstances. After fifty-five years of recurring tumors and horrendous pain, God made me whole. In a spirit of celebration, I removed my vehicle's handicap placard from the rearview mirror. But then I found myself negotiating a medical bill while waiting in my car. "I'm so sorry you've been ill," the lady soothed. *You've got her where you want her, Roberta,* an inner voice whispered. *She feels sorry for you. You'll get a break on that bill.* But noticing my handicap placard on the floor was an eye-opener. I'd said goodbye to it. It was time to bid the sick Roberta a fond farewell too. And say a passionate hello to God's new me.

—Roberta

Be with me, Lord, in all of life's goodbyes. Amen.

success

Commit your actions to the Lord, and your plans will succeed.
—Proverbs 16:3 NLT

During my senior year in high school, my classmates voted me "most likely to succeed." The title usually went to the boy and girl who others believed would do well in life, the ones who would make a name for themselves, earn lots of money, and enjoy an illustrious career. I've achieved neither great fame nor fortune. Maybe my classmates will ask for a recount?

While I've had goals, I can honestly say that I've never had a master plan. I just take life step by step and make the most of the opportunities that come my way. For me, true success is obeying God's voice, having love and peace, helping others, and appreciating the blessing of family, friends, and good health. As my octogenarian mom often says, "What else is there?"

—Barbranda

Dear Lord, help me to keep my eyes on You, and guide me in Your path of success. Amen.

warmth

The consciousness of loving and being loved brings a warmth and richness to life that nothing else can bring.
—Oscar Wilde

M y husband, Mike, is a hugger. "Bring it in," he says, when he wants to give out a hug. A long-lasting, tight, warm embrace. There's nothing better than one of those hugs, and I measure all others by the ones I get from Mike.

In my world, there's little better than the warmth from those hugs. Or the sun on my face, the text from a friend—"just thinking about you"—and the heat of the fire as Mike and I sit outside on the patio under the stars on a summer night.

For me, warmth equates to love, contentment, and safety.
—Carolyn

Dear Lord, let me not forget to give others the same amount of warmth and love I receive. Amen.

hold

God holds me in the palm of His hand and
no one can take Him from me.
—Francine Rivers

M y daughter is an adult now, but when she was a toddler, she would often amble to me or her mother with arms outstretched, saying plaintively, "Hold me?" Her plea was adorable and irresistible, and my wife and I grieved a little when she outgrew it.

How often have I stretched out my arms and heart to God with a similar plea? Sometimes I can only—and repeatedly—plead, "Hold me?" But I can say with the psalmist, "Where can I go from your Spirit? Where can I flee from your presence?...If I rise on the wings of the dawn, if I settle on the far side of the sea, even there your hand will guide me, your right hand will hold me fast" (Ps. 139:7–10 NIV).

—Bob

Father, hold me. Amen.

ritual

It seemed to be a necessary ritual that he should prepare himself for sleep by meditating under the solemnity of the night sky...a mysterious transaction between the infinity of the soul and the infinity of the universe.
—Victor Hugo

'm a creature of habit. Every day at 11:00 a.m. I make myself a cup of tea (steeped for four minutes) and a frosted brown sugar cinnamon Pop-Tart (toasted for twenty seconds in the office microwave, twenty-four seconds in the microwave at home). It's a habit that almost feels like a ritual. So much so that I looked up the difference. Turns out, any habit can become a ritual. The key is intention. Four minutes of tea-steeping time can turn into four minutes of daily meditation; and twenty seconds is plenty of time to find three things I'm thankful for.
—Meg

God, help me take comfort in daily rituals and find ways to honor You in them. Amen.

stir

A gentle answer turns away wrath, but a harsh
word stirs up anger.
—Proverbs 15:1 NIV

M uch as I hate to admit it, I once loved to "stir the pot," and I'm not talking about a big vat of chili. As a member of my high school debate team, I learned to spar with words. I argued for the sake of arguing. My words were often more cutting than kind.

Decades later, social media exacerbated my bad habit. I could stir things up not only with people I knew, but also with total strangers. For a while, it gave me a rush of pleasure to "win" arguments on Facebook. Until it didn't. What was the point in trying to prove others wrong? In trying to show how clever or well-informed I was? In making people feel hurt and angry? There was no point. So I stopped.

My goal these days? To stir only feelings of harmony, joy, and love.

—Jennie

Lord, make me an instrument of Your peace. Amen.

remember

Those who cannot remember the past are
condemned to repeat it.
—George Santayana

My son, Isaac, who was born with Down syndrome, is my oft-cited object lesson in remembering. Isaac reminds me of God's faithfulness and how things that seem challenging at the time can truly prove to be the greatest blessing ever. I also remember the countless other times I conjured an elaborate catastrophe in my head that turned out to be nothing. I remember how bad I feel when I eat three bowls of pasta, or conversely, how great I feel when I honor my daily jogging habit no matter what. Recently, I remembered how I've deeply regretted not expressing my true feelings with loved ones, stuffing them down, missing out on growing intimacy. Remembering is powerful. I want always to remember.

—Isabella

*Dear God, help me remember the lessons learned—
the good and the bad. Amen.*

inclusion

Beloved, if God so loved us, we also ought
to love one another.
—1 John 4:11 ESV

G rowing up, Thanksgiving was always a special time.
Every year we'd pack up the car and head to New
Jersey to visit with our close family friends, Ted and
Jane, who shared a love of people and travel. As they met and
connected with folks around the world, Ted and Jane included
new friends in their lives, often at Thanksgiving.

One year, a musician whom Ted and Jane met while on
a botany trip to the Amazon rain forest in Brazil joined the
Thanksgiving feast. He had an uncanny ability to turn any ordinary object into a musical instrument, including forks, couches,
body parts, TVs, and other items. What an orchestra! It wasn't
"traditional" music, but we all had a great time together because the musician shared his gifts with us.

—John

*God grant me the gift of bringing people together to love,
work, and honor You. Amen.*

cross

There is no cross, big or small, in our life which the
Lord does not share with us.
—Pope Francis

———————

Like many others, I live with a chronic condition. When I
first received the diagnosis, my stomach tightened, and I
fought panic. I couldn't fathom coping with an illness for
the rest of my life, let alone taking medications and altering
my lifestyle. But if I wanted my body to remain a temple fit for
Christ, I'd need to do both. It was my personal cross to bear.

As time has passed, I've learned to adjust to this challenge.
Supportive and understanding family and friends lighten the
load. But the Lord slips my cross onto His shoulder and carries
this burden daily. He shares every one of the crosses in my life.

—Heidi

Jesus, thank You for being with me and for sharing
the weight of all my "crosses." Amen.

dunamis

Now to him who is able to do immeasurably
more than all we ask or imagine, according to
his power that is at work within us.
—Ephesians 3:20 NIV

'm old enough to remember the character J.J. on the television sitcom *Good Times*. Played by comedian and actor Jimmy Walker, J.J. electrified audiences with his signature exclamation, "Dy-no-mite!" Walker and "Dy-no-mite" were key factors in the popularity of the show.

"Dy-no-mite" is at work in every Christian's life, and I pray it often for myself and others. I don't use Jimmy Walker's pronunciation, but I sometimes use the Greek word *dunamis*, which is typically translated in the Bible as "power." It's also the source of the English word *dynamite*, and that association enriches my praying. I ask often for God's *dunamis* to permeate and energize my life and the lives of those around me—a prayer with explosive power.

—Bob

Mighty God, show Your dunamis today in my life and in the lives
of those around me. Amen.

standby

Truly, I say to you, unless you turn and become like children,
you will never enter the kingdom of heaven.
—Matthew 18:3 ESV

Back in the early seventies, when a television station had a signal problem, a horizontal, colored pattern would appear on screen with a message that read: "Please stand by." One day when my sisters and I were watching TV, the "Please stand by" message appeared on screen. My younger sister, Ellen, who was five years old and a new reader, got up from the floor where she was sitting and stood by the TV. With smiles, my older sister, Georgia, and I asked Ellen what she was doing. She looked at us earnestly and said, "I'm standing by!"

Ellen had taken literally the words that she'd read and immediately did what they said. What a lovely reminder for me to do the same with God's Word.

—Janet

Lord, with the same childlike faith and obedience that
Ellen had, help me to trust and obey Your Word. Amen.

redemption

The cost of redemption cannot be overstated. The wonders of grace cannot be overemphasized. Christ took the hell he didn't deserve so we could have the heaven we don't deserve.
—Randy Alcorn

When I was a child, my mother collected S&H Green Stamps. Do you remember them? Customers earned them with purchases at selected merchants, such as grocery stores, and collected them in books into which they pasted the gummed stamps.

I grew up in church, so I was familiar with the term *redemption* as a Christian belief. But why did my mother "redeem" her stamps to get items in the S&H catalogue?

Eventually I made the connection using the dictionary, where the first definition is "to buy back: repurchase." Because Jesus saw me as precious, He redeemed me by trading His life for mine, much as (on a minuscule scale) my mom *redeemed* her collected stamps in return for something she felt was precious.

—Jon

Jesus, thank You for Your incredible act of redemption. Amen.

presence

And we have known and believed the love that God has for us. God is love, and he who abides in love abides in God, and God in him.
—1 John 4:16 NKJV

Auntie Margaret, we called her. Not an aunt, not even a cousin, but a beloved church friend and neighbor. We gave her a ride every Sunday morning. My wife, Carol, and I would rush off to choir rehearsal, and Auntie Margaret would get things ready for coffee hour or a Bible study or the soup kitchen. She was ever-present. When we complimented her, calling her a pillar of the church, she pooh-poohed us. Once, when I woke up from a medical procedure and found her sitting by my bedside, I knew I was going to be okay. Her presence spoke love.

—Rick

God, I feel Your presence—and when I turn to those I love, those who have always stuck by me, Your presence is in their presence. When they show up, You show up. Amen.

believe

Believe in yourself! Have faith in your abilities! Without a humble but reasonable confidence in your own powers you cannot be successful or happy.
—Norman Vincent Peale

believe in you." I stared, speechless, after Kevin gave me a serious look and spoke those words. Words I'd never heard before, from anyone. I was cleaning out my college dorm room and heading home for summer break. I told Kev I wasn't sure I'd finish in time to attend his best friend's graduation. Kevin and I hadn't started dating yet—we'd begun our friendship only four months earlier. But when those four words reached my ears, something almost magical and luminous burst inside my heart. *I can do this*, I thought. *If Kevin believes I can, well, then I believe I can, too.* We recently celebrated our forty-fifth anniversary. Because we still believe in each other.
—Jeanette

Lord, I am Your child. Because You are with me, for me, and in me, I believe in myself. Amen.

desert

You know that the testing of your faith produces steadfastness.
—James 1:3 NIV

I drove the rental car south through the gathering evening, air conditioner rattling complaint. Israel—the Negev. Let me tell you, when God breathed this little patch of geography into existence, He made *desert*.

Broken. Empty.

Like me.

Ahead, great clouds of dust rose up. As I got closer, I saw military tanks training. That resonated. How many times have I been taken into the "desert" to prepare for spiritual battles to come? And here I was again.

But then…God.

The western sky turned gold, purple, then a riot of stars. Awed, I pulled over and got out. I stood there, drunk with majestic light. It hit me—this place was not empty. It was overflowing with *Him*. I breathed deep. Whispered thanks. Sometimes the desert isn't a trial at all. It's simply a moment to be still and be loved.

—Buck

Thank You, Lord, that Your arm is forever around my shoulder.
Amen.

retreat

Nowhere can man find a quieter or more untroubled
retreat than in his own soul.
—Marcus Aurelius

Years ago I did a meditation retreat. A silent meditation retreat. Ten days—no speaking. It was one thing to retreat from everyday life, but withdrawing into total silence? Everyone said I'd be bored. Empty. Lonely. Years later, you know what my most vivid memory of those ten days is? My dreams. Dreams richer and grander than any before, or since. Like the night I dreamed I was floating on a dark sea, looking up at a sky full of stars, the only sound being the quiet roll of the ocean. In retreating from the outside world, I discovered an amazing world within.

—Meg

God, thank You for the quiet moments. Don't let me forget that whenever I retreat into solitude, You are there waiting for me. Amen.

listen

Most people do not listen with the intent to understand;
they listen with the intent to reply.
—Stephen Covey

To hear my father tell it, God talked to him constantly, in a booming Old Testament voice. It bugged me, because though I thought I was listening, I never heard the Almighty even whisper to me. Then I signed up to be a Stephen Minister. The program matches participants with people going through a rough patch for weekly sessions. "Your job isn't to talk, but to listen," the trainer said. It occurred to me, that's what I'd been doing with God. I'd been talking up a storm to Him, but listening, really quieting my mind and hearing Him speak? Not so much. The difference was amazing, as if an entire world had been opened up to me, simply by learning to listen.

—Evan

Lord, help me to talk less and listen more. Amen.

longevity

My son, do not forget my teaching, but keep my commands
in your heart, for they will prolong your life many years and
bring you peace and prosperity.
—Proverbs 3:1–2 NIV

I have been reading about different people groups and their
longevity. In one small Italian village, there are over three
hundred centenarians. Nearly a third of their population is
over one hundred years old. The scientists think their longevity
is caused by a mix of genes, lifestyle, and diet.

Longevity seems like a mystery. I often find myself worn out
by the stress of daily living. *How can I live a long and healthy
life?* God already knows how many days I have on this earth. My
longevity is anchored in Him. Following His loving commands,
centering my life in His words of hope, brings peace and long
life. Abiding in Him is good for body and soul.

—Susanna

*Thank You for giving me life. Show me how to anchor
myself in Your loving words all of my days. Amen.*

save

God our Savior...wants all people to be saved and to come to a knowledge of the truth.
—1 Timothy 2:3–4 NIV

Years ago, I was halfway through a book-length writing project when my computer's hard drive crashed. I tried everything I could think of to revive it, but nothing worked. I took it to my computer guru and left it in his hands. It was a crisis, but not a catastrophe because I was obsessive about saving my work, backing up documents every noon, quitting time, and end-of-week. My saving habit was my salvation, so to speak.

According to the Bible, God is passionate about saving too. He "wants all people to be saved and to come to a knowledge of the truth" (1 Tim. 2:4 NIV). We are all a work in progress, and He is constantly working (see John 5:17) to help and heal, save and sanctify, strengthen and supply.

—Bob

God my Savior, accomplish Your saving work in and through me this day. Amen.

near

"Am I a God who is near," declares the Lord,
"And not a God far off?"
—Jeremiah 23:23 NASB

On one foggy winter morning, since I had been having some heart irregularity episodes, I asked my husband not to leave on his errands. I wanted him near. As a child at a church picnic I chased after a car, crying, because it looked like ours and I thought my parents had forgotten me. I wanted them near. It's especially this way with Jesus. I want Him near. He promises to live in me through His Holy Spirit when I receive Him into my life. I carry His presence. I am so much more than myself. To know He is near—to practice His nearness—is to be filled with the pleasure of God.

—Carol

Jesus, every day You are near! Amen.

honesty

Honesty and transparency make you vulnerable. Be honest
and transparent anyway.
—Mother Teresa

After my divorce two decades ago, an editor encouraged me to write about it. I had serious misgivings for I feared people would judge me for my perceived failures. "No, Roberta," he urged. "If you'll just be honest, people will love you even more." As hard as it was, I bared my heart and soul and told my truth. I wrote how renovating a hundred-year-old log cabin with God by my side actually renovated *me*. Those writings generated absolutely no hate mail but rather an outpouring of caring and kindness that strengthened my spirit. I'd never felt so free. Still today, people remember my battle-scarred words, reminding me of how honesty actually empowered me. As one dear reader wrote recently: "Being vulnerable, Roberta, never costs us as much as it gives."

—Roberta

Give me the courage, Lord, to be vulnerable and honest. Amen.

stillness

Be still, and know that I am God; I will be exalted
among the nations, I will be exalted in the earth.
—Psalm 46:10 NIV

When my life doesn't add up the way I want, I become
the great mathematician. I try to make calculated
decisions. Stillness is usually not included in the
equation, especially when I don't have clarity, so I spend all my
energy trying to make sense of God's subtractions and divisions
by attempting to add and multiply. The problem is, I can never
outwit God's intended equation for my life. He's far beyond
my calculus. Yet, as I try to make sense of life's challenges, I'm
learning to rest in the stillness of God and His infinite wisdom.

—Ty'Ann

*Heavenly Father, teach me to be still in the midst of upheaval and
unclarity. Your results are always better than mine. Amen.*

lovely

Finally, brothers and sisters, whatever is true, whatever
is noble, whatever is right, whatever is pure, whatever is
lovely, whatever is admirable—if anything is excellent or
praiseworthy—think about such things.
—Philippians 4:8 NIV

Moving away and starting college was hard. I started to doubt my decision to attend college four hours away from home. I was homesick and nervous about making new friends. A few weeks in, I was approached by a student in the student center who offered a friendly smile and welcoming conversation. Before we parted ways, she added quickly, "By the way, my name is Lovely." Of course, this sweet girl's name was Lovely!

Over the next couple of months, I discovered more lovely people, administrators, teachers, students, and friends. As I focused on such things, I realized that maybe my choice of college wasn't wrong after all.

—Jaylin

*Lord, help me to realize all the lovely things
You set in place for me. Amen.*

close

Why do you look at the speck that is in your brother's eye?
—Matthew 7:3 NASB

Funny how words can mean different things depending on the situation. Take the word *close*, for example. When my wife puts her arms around me, close is good. When a guy wedges into the seat next to me on an airplane and I get a big whiff of his dead rat breath, it's not.

"Really, God?"

God laughs. "You think your breath is better?"

Close. I love the fact that as we draw near to God, He shatters every definition of that word. With Him, close is encompassing, saturating. He is with me and through me and *in* me. He loves.

And convicts.

"Hi, I'm Buck," I say to my seatmate.

He just smiles and offers me a stick of gum.

—Buck

Lord, thank You for always be close to us. Amen.

yield

Being filled with the Spirit is simply this—having my whole nature yielded to His power.
—Andrew Murray

The triangular red-and-white traffic sign instructed me to give way to other vehicles, allowing them to go first. I was in a hurry and reluctant to wait my turn but was aware that disregarding the sign could result in an accident, which risked injury to my passengers and those in the other cars.

Spiritually speaking, I might also be reluctant to yield to God's plans and timing in my life because of my own desires. But yielding to Him—trusting Him to "work in us what is pleasing to Him" (Heb. 13:21 NIV)—is what allows me to do His will and try to bring Him glory at every turn.

—Kirsten

Holy Spirit, I yield to Your work in my life, asking You to accomplish Your purposes in and through me. Amen.

anyway

Yet I will rejoice in the LORD, I will be joyful in God my Savior.
—Habakkuk 3:18 NIV

When my kids were teenagers, they got into the habit of shrugging and saying "whatever." I hit on an answer I considered much better: "Anyway." "Whatever" signaled indifference; "anyway" signified determination. "Whatever" implied helplessness; "anyway" indicated strength. "Whatever" suggested stagnation; "anyway" denoted motion.

The ancient prophet Habakkuk wrote the book of the Bible that bears his name at a time when violence, injustice, and oppression afflicted his nation, Judah, and its people. In it, he prayed what I've learned to call an "anyway prayer." Foreseeing a series of unfortunate circumstances (crop failure, famine, poverty), he said, "Yet I will rejoice in the LORD, I will be joyful in God my Savior" (Hab. 3:18 NIV).

"Anyway" is amazingly simple and surprisingly therapeutic. It allows me to acknowledge the challenges of the moment (or near future) while encouraging a faith-filled response: "Anyway."

—Bob

Lord, whatever happens, I will rejoice in You anyway. Amen.

differences

Our similarities bring us to a common ground; our differences allow us to be fascinated by each other.
—Tom Robbins

I scrolled through photos of the home my daughter's best friend purchased. Every room was shockingly bright: yellow, turquoise, purple, orange. How many coats of primer would it take to tame such outrageous colors? Did the previous owners actually like their choices? They apparently didn't care about Pantone's color of the year or the designers' picks on home-improvement TV. Maybe they were artists who enjoyed vibrant hues. What would they think of the light gray that would soon cover each wall, the very opposite of colorful? I marveled at the contrast between my taste and theirs. Were their personalities as lively as their color choices? Suddenly I imagined sitting in their yellow kitchen, enjoying conversation over a cup of coffee, unaware of our differences.

—Karen

Father, teach me to embrace the differences in others, to recognize our similarities, and to remember we are all Your children. Amen.

hero

God has my admiration, I admire all He has done,
is doing and will do. He is my Hero!
—Lola Garcia

When I was six years old, almost seven, I feared lightning and thunder. One night, I ran into my parents' room, hoping to sleep in their bed. My mother said, "No, no, no! You have your own room. Go pray to God. He'll listen to you." Obediently, I went back to my room, kneeled down on my bedside, folded my hands, and started to pray. Before I said "Amen," the storm ended. God heard my prayer, and He answered! Yay, God! I was in awe and wanted to know all that I could about this Hero who had heard my tiny prayer and stopped the storm.

—Didi

Heavenly Father, thank You for always listening. Thank You for being the ever-present Hero in my life. Amen.

faith

Faith sees the invisible, believes the unbelievable, and receives the impossible.
—Corrie ten Boom

Like my dad, I'm a born dreamer. I still see him seated at his desk, his gaze distant, slight smile on his lips. Now my husband witnesses that same look as he watches me drift to faraway places in my head. I can't help it—it's in my genes. Daddy taught me to believe dreams can come true. My Heavenly Father convinced me that with faith, anything is possible (see Matt. 19:26). I've learned faith triumphs over dreams.

Jesus has deepened our relationship, blessing me with a home, loved ones, and a career that honors Him. As I grew in the truth, I received what seemed impossible. Forgiveness. Eternal life. Hope. I understand the power of faith. I can touch it on my daughter's face, smell it in the roses gracing my garden, and read it in the Bible. It's real. It's forever. And it's mine.

—Heidi

Lord, thank you for making my faith real. Amen.

poiema

We have become his poetry.
—Ephesians 2:10 TPT

O ne of my favorite college classes covered many different forms of English poetry, from free verse and blank
verse to sonnets, sestinas, villanelles, and more. We
read a variety of poetry, and while I didn't fall in love with all
of it, I've enjoyed reading several books of poetry every year
since.

So I was delighted to learn the deeper meaning of the verse
in Ephesians 2 that says of Jesus's followers, "we are God's handiwork" (Eph. 2:10 NIV). The Greek word that is usually translated
as "handiwork" or "masterpiece" is *poiema*. From it comes
the English word *poem*. What a lovely word picture it paints of
God's people as a poem God is writing! It's become one of my
favorite prayers to pray for myself and others, recognizing that
we are each God's poiema.

—Bob

Lord, make a beautiful poem of the lives we live. Amen.

blossom

Blossom by blossom the spring begins.
—Algernon Charles Swinburne

This winter was my first in Idaho. Coming from Northern California's mild climate, the sharp wind and brisk snows felt new. Trees lost every single leaf. Bare branches stood in stark relief against the steel-gray sky. For months, it seemed like I was living in a black-and-white Ansel Adams print. Then the craziest thing happened. *Spring!* Within days, Adams's muted grays were replaced by Monet's sun-kissed pinks and vibrant greens. The tulip trees lining our streets were heavy with rose-colored and white blossoms, full of hope and promise. Their transformation reminded me of my own. My heart often feels barren and dark in the midst of life's difficult moments. But bathed in the warmth of God's love, new life springs up. His presence brings hope and healing. His grace causes a blossoming of the soul.

—Susanna

God, thank You for Your life-giving love. Let it cause the withered parts of my soul to blossom with grace and hope. Amen.

relief

What happiness for those whose guilt has been
forgiven! What joys when sins are covered over! What
relief for those who have confessed their sins and God has
cleared their record.
—Psalm 32:1–2 TLB

I still remember feeling like a failure in my first job. Some of
my failings were imagined. Many were real. I made so many
typos that my documents looked like mountains of Wite-Out
correction fluid (remember typewriters?). I put in more than
eight hours every day, but I never accomplished all that my
boss needed done. When I could no longer stand the pressure,
I told her I knew I wasn't keeping up and perhaps I should start
looking for another job.

"It's okay," she said. "I'm at fault too. I haven't spent time
showing you the ropes. You need to reduce the typos, but
there are other things I can help you with. Let's start over."
What a relief!

—Michelle

*Dear Father, help me to remember that You are always ready to
clear my record. Amen.*

abide

Abide in Me, and I in you.
—John 15:4 NKJV

My granddaughter Calleigh copes daily with cystic fibrosis (CF). At seven years old, she was admitted to the hospital for the first time so her body could fight off an infection. Though she and her younger brother (who also has CF) had visited the hospital many times for outpatient treatments, she was understandably fearful, until her mother assured her, "I will be with you." Calleigh asked, "The whole time?" Mom answered, "Even while you sleep." Calleigh said, "And I'll be with you."

That's what it means to abide. Jesus said, "I am the vine, you are the branches. He who abides in Me, and I in him, bears much fruit; for without Me you can do nothing" (John 15:5 NKJV). Like Henry Lyte, who penned the hymn, "Abide with Me," we can face life's struggles and even death's approach with the prayer "abide" on our lips and in our hearts.

—Bob

Helper of the helpless, oh, abide with me. Amen.

admire

Let your conversation be always full of grace, seasoned with salt, so that you may know how to answer everyone.
—Colossians 4:6 NIV

When we moved from LA to rural Illinois twenty years ago, I left behind several close friends. Including my prayer partner, Kathy. The princess of diplomacy, Kathy had the gift of changing painful confrontations into messages of kindness and encouragement: "Look a little closer at this dim corner—I see a sunbeam in it." As an Irish redhead with the gift of (too much) gab, I admired my friend's flair for using words to soothe and offer hope. Thanks to Kathy's influence, my own way of handling tough situations changed—from blurting out something without thinking to listening for God's wisdom in my heart. I never told Kathy how much I admired her, how much she helped me grow up. Until now.

—Jeanette

Dear Lord, use my words to lift up, not tear down.
And to tell others when I admire them. Amen.

morsel

Better is a dry morsel and quietness with it
than a house full of feasting with strife.
—Proverbs 17:1 NASB

A morsel is just a bite. Something small. When I cared for my centenarian aunt, she said one day, "You are a precious morsel in the hands of the Lord." She had dementia. Didn't realize I was her niece. But she recognized kindness. That moment I happened to be bringing her a cup of morning coffee. Her words lodged in my heart. "A precious morsel." The more I thought about being a precious morsel, the more I understood that that is all I really want to be. A bit of love. A sliver of wisdom. A scrap of joy. A thread of encouragement. Little acts that in the Lord's faithful hands become precious morsels that go down sweet.

—Carol

You, Lord, are a big God who delights in small things. Amen.

promise

Sovereign LORD, you are God! Your covenant is trustworthy, and you have promised these good things to your servant.
—2 Samuel 7:28 NIV

Before I got married, I remember shuddering at all the promises I'd have to make in the wedding ceremony: "for better, for worse, for richer, for poorer, in sickness and in health, to love and to cherish, till death do us part." How would I ever keep a huge commitment like that? One friend half jokingly said that he'd mutter to himself, "for richer, please, for richer." Who wants to promise to do the harder stuff? And yet, here I am, some thirty-five years later, happily wed to my beloved wife. We made our vows, in the presence of family and friends, and before God—and He's surely helped us keep those promises in all of life's struggles and blessings.

—Rick

God, You give the promise of eternal life, today, tomorrow, forever. We can only keep our promises to one another because of Your greater promise. Amen.

yes

The lines have fallen to me in pleasant places;
yes, I have a good inheritance.
—Psalm 16:6 NKJV

A s I pushed my two-year-old granddaughter in a swing, her bright red hair blew back and forth, sometimes covering, sometimes uncovering her face. Then she threw back her head, turned her face to the sky, closed her eyes, and said, "Yes!" She said it repeatedly, with each new push. "Yes!" to the joy of the moment. "Yes!" to the sun's warmth on her face. "Yes!" to the rush of wind past her ears.

It was a special moment, and not just because she is my grandchild. It inspired me to pray.

That evening as I retired to my prayer chair in my study, I leaned my head back against the chair. I closed my eyes. I pictured one of the day's many blessings: "Yes!" Again, I visualized another beautiful moment: "Yes!" And another: "Yes!"

—Bob

Father, I say yes to Your many blessings and mercies today.
Amen.

no

The oldest, shortest words—"yes" and "no"—are those
which require the most thought.
—Pythagoras

I hear a siren in the distance, signaling some emergency. I say,
"No." In other words, "Don't let the worst happen. Let no
one be hurt. Prevent or heal disease or disaster."

I drive through town, and I see a stately old church building,
spray painted with hateful words and racist graffiti. I pray, "No."

I see a tragedy or injustice reported on television or the
Internet: "No." An animal squeals in pain: "No." A car speeds
past, well over the speed limit: "No."

"No." A single syllable. But one of my (new) favorite ways to
pray. In spite of—or perhaps because of—its brevity, it connects
me quickly and effectively to my gracious God, who knows my
heart and exactly what I mean when I say "No."

—Bob

*Lord, help me to say "no" today to everything that is contrary
to Your good, perfect, and pleasing will. Amen.*

merciful

Blessed are the merciful, for they will be shown mercy.
—Matthew 5:7 NIV

My favorite vocabulary activity as a middle-school English teacher was having my students complete word studies. They would research the etymology of words like literary detectives, uncovering the root words and deeper meanings. Their discoveries thrilled my nerdy teacher's soul. The etymology of the word *mercy* is multilayered. *Merriam-Webster* says it was first used in thirteenth-century Medieval Latin and meant "price paid" or "wages." It shares the same root as "merchandise" and the French word for "thanks" (*merci*).

This new, deeper meaning of *mercy* leaves me undone. How great was Jesus's mercy, that He paid the price for my sin? With His sacrifice, He bought my freedom from death and purchased me new life! There is no one more merciful than He is. And when I follow in His footsteps, being merciful to those around me, I am truly blessed.

—Susanna

Jesus, thank You, thank You, thank You, for being merciful to me. Amen.

liberty

My mother raised me, and then freed me.
—Maya Angelou

A s college graduation approached, two choices became clear. I could pursue a traditional career path via a well-paid job in my major, at a top-tier company with promising advancement opportunities. I'd be near home and would be a significant, financial help to our family (my sister still in college and our mom a single parent). Or I could accept a modest-paying position with a growing ministry organization about 2,500 miles from home. My mother released me from any expectation or obligation to select option one for her or my sister's benefit. She encouraged me to do whatever I thought best. Despite prior sacrifices on my behalf, my mother gave me the liberty to choose. Her selflessness set me free and I was grateful. After carefully considering everything, I selected option two. I'm still convinced it was the right decision.

—Steve

Thank You, Lord, for the liberty to make choices in my life every day. Amen.

messy

People, even more than things, have to be restored,
renewed, revived, reclaimed, and redeemed;
never throw out anyone.
—Audrey Hepburn

While going through old correspondence, I came across a letter from an out-of-town friend who had once visited me. "Your darling cabin tells the story in treasures of the woman who lives there," she'd written. Her words were all it took to pick the lock on *that* memory.

These days, my cabin was a total mess. What had once been a soulful smattering of objects was now a cloud of chaos beyond redemption. I was dealing with the aftermath of decades of illness and my inability to keep up with the place. I was both mortified by its condition and overwhelmed by all that needed to be done. Just then my sister Rebekkah appeared on the scene. "Don't fret, Pet," she told me. "It has to get better. You gotta have the messy before the magic."

—Roberta

I'm trusting You, Lord, to turn my mess into Your marvelous.
Again. Amen.

relax

The time to relax is when you don't have time for it.
—Sydney J. Harris

Several days a week I try to take Rusty, my nine-year-old, slightly overweight sheltie, for a short walk. But it's often an exercise in frustration. My idea of a walk is getting from point A to point B in the shortest possible amount of time. Rusty likes to sniff one patch of grass after another. How different can grass really smell? But the other day I decided to let Rusty control the pace, letting him sniff to his heart's content. The walk took nearly twice as long, but what a wondrous experience. The sounds of birds. Wind rustling through the leaves. A kind of natural symphony, every note God's creation. One I never heard when I was hoofing it. I've noticed that Rusty spends most of his day relaxing and seems perfectly contented. I'm thinking he's onto something.

—Evan

Lord, help me to relax and appreciate the wonder of Your universe. Amen.

color

The heavens declare the glory of God; the skies proclaim the work of his hands.
—Psalm 19:1 NIV

There is a field at the top of Pleasant Hill that takes my breath away. It's actually not the field—it's the sky above it. Driving past it when my children were little, I'd often exclaim, "Oh, look at the pretty picture God has painted for us in the sky!" Now I say that to my granddaughter. I stop the car and open the window, and we name the colors that we see. A sunrise of orange and red. An afternoon with blue sky, white clouds, and yellow sun. A purple-and-pink sunset. God could have picked dull colors for the world, but instead He chose to paint the skies with brilliant hues. Those colors ignite my heart with praise for the Master Artist.

—Becky

God, thank You for surrounding me with color. Amen.

blue

A certain blue enters your soul.
—Henri Matisse

I love blue, and I'm not alone. A recent study involving two thousand people asked for their favorite color, and blue won hands down, regardless of gender.

It certainly is among the most expressive of colors, covering a wide variety of emotions. Blue is calming. Yet when I feel blue, I'm down. But a blue sky brings feelings of endless possibility and hope. Blue has endless variations that are instantly recognizable: baby blue, robin's-egg blue, sky blue, midnight blue, navy blue, royal blue, not to mention named variations such as ultramarine, cerulean, azure, cobalt, and more.

What is your shade of blue right now? Is it the midnight blue of sorrow or the sunny azure of an exciting new day? Know that no matter which one it is, God will walk with you in that blue today, sharing your pain, sharing your joy, because He cares for you.

—Jon

Dear Lord, thank You for being with me, no matter the circumstance. Amen.

suddenly

Suddenly an angel of the Lord appeared and a light shone
in the cell. He struck Peter on the side and woke him up.
"Quick, get up!" he said, and the chains fell off Peter's wrists.
—Acts 12:7 NIV

We'd wanted to move to Florida, but the timing wasn't
right. Then I started a business and wanted to stay
put. Then the business floundered, but we couldn't
sell our house. Then *suddenly*, in a matter of weeks, we rented
our house, packed up, and moved to Florida, everything falling
into place.

In the verse above, Peter is in jail, shackled, with scant
prospects of getting out, when suddenly an angel clears his
path to escape and he's free. Suddenly! Over the years I've
complained a lot about waiting, but now I know that at any
time God can intervene again—suddenly.

—Isabella

*Abba, help me to deal patiently with the tedium of waiting so
that when You intervene suddenly, I can be ready to go! Amen.*

prepare

Preparation time is never wasted time.
—Anonymous

M y (now adult) children have long ridiculed me for my penchant for preparation. Each evening I set out my coffeepot and breakfast dishes for the next morning. I lay out the next day's clothes. I check tire pressure before a long drive. And so on. My kids tease me, and I tease back, as they do similar things now that they are adults.

What does the future hold? What lies ahead? We may suspect, but we never really know. So, a word from the Twenty-Third Psalm can serve us well, whether we expect good things or hard things ahead. The psalmist sang, "You prepare a table before me" (Ps. 23:5 NIV). Whatever may come our way, the word *prepare* invites our Shepherd to go ahead, even "in the presence of my enemies," and remove obstacles, defend against dangers, and make straight paths for our feet (see Prov. 4:11).

—Bob

*Lord, please prepare me for whatever today—
and tomorrow—holds. Amen.*

spring

And He will come to us like the rain,
as the spring rain waters the earth.
—Hosea 6:3 NASB

My wife loves springtime in northern Idaho. Me, not so much. Especially when I'm building a fire in the wood-stove and it's almost June. I'm ready for a barbecue and a beach. After all, I survived winter—is a little sun too much to ask?

Life has its seasons. Some comfortable, others far from it. But, as my wife will tell you, all are necessary. How many times have I emerged from some dark valley ready to charge the mountain? But, like the good Father He is, God knows I'm not ready. He pulls me into His arms and stills me. He waters and nurtures and heals. Then, only then, He places me gently into the sun.

The rain is gone in Idaho now. It's supposed to hit ninety today.

Time to mow all that spring grass.

—Buck

Thank You for life's seasons. Even the long spring! Amen.

masterpiece

For we are God's masterpiece.
—Ephesians 2:10 NLT

A few times each summer, my husband pulls out the old-fashioned ice-cream maker and his mother's recipe for a family-favorite tradition. He measures the ingredients, pours them in, and begins to turn the crank. That's right. No electric ice-cream maker here. He insists the only way to create a masterpiece is to do the work by hand. So he churns by hand, keeping a steady rhythm, watching frost appear at the bottom of the metal cylinder and move up as the ice cream forms. As he churns, he feels the ingredients thicken until the cold treat reaches the perfect consistency. Then he serves the ice cream in Styrofoam cups with plastic spoons—a family legacy, a labor of love, a masterpiece.

—Karen

Father, thank You for making me a labor of love, for patiently molding me into the masterpiece You plan for me to become. Amen.

forever

Jesus Christ is the same yesterday and today and forever.
—Hebrews 13:8 NIV

For years my husband and I loved living in a resort town. We had good jobs, a beautiful home, and wonderful friends. Excitedly, we returned for a few days to visit our old friends and hangouts. But as we drove into town, we got lost. It seemed the streets and buildings had multiplied. The businesses we'd frequented had changed hands. And most of our friends had relocated. Our house was no longer the sweet place we'd called home. The changes were huge and left us devastated.

Driving home, we spoke of our disappointment and realized that even though we hadn't noticed, we, too, had changed a lot over the years. The only thing in our lives that remained the same was the Lord. He alone is eternal and unchanging. I can depend on Him now and forever.

—Heidi

Jesus, thank You for being the One I can depend on to always be there for me. Amen.

teleios

When we get away from self to God, there all is truth and purity and holiness, and our heart finds peace, wisdom, completeness, delight, joy, victory.
—Charles Spurgeon

G randma's egg noodles were a highlight of holiday meals at her farmhouse. But this time she shook her head. "They're just not right. I feel like I forgot something." We insisted they were as good as ever, but Grandma continued to puzzle over it. Finally, she began laughing hysterically. Regaining her composure, she said, "I remember what I left out. Eggs! I forgot the eggs!"

The goal of the Christian life, the Bible says, is to "become mature, attaining to the whole measure of the fullness of Christ (Eph. 4:13 NIV). The Greek word translated "mature" is *teleios*, a state in which nothing is left out or lacking. *Teleios* is what I pray, often, for myself, and my brothers and sisters in the faith—that we find completion in Jesus, lacking nothing.

—Bob

Lord, let teleios characterize the lives of me and my brothers and sisters in the faith. Amen.

yet

Yet I will rejoice in the LORD.
—Habakkuk 3:18 NIV

M y problem still isn't solved," I lamented to my friend. "It just hasn't worked out." She smiled and replied with a single word: "Yet." Her response caught me completely off guard. I opened my mouth to rebut, but no words came. She was right—I had no idea when or how God might act. He might have been mere moments away from answering my prayer. Or He might have provided a different solution than the one I'd been asking for. Even one that, from my human vantage point, didn't feel like a solution at all. No matter what He did or didn't do, or how difficult my circumstances were, that little three-letter word, *yet*, asked me to rejoice either way, simply because of who He is: my Savior and my strength.

—Kirsten

Thank You, Father, for being a reason for joy in all circumstances. Amen.

expect

In the morning, LORD, you hear my voice; in the morning
I lay my requests before you and wait expectantly.
—Psalm 5:3 NIV

The rain woke us, pounding on the roof overhead. My three-year-old granddaughter, Sadie, and I had a full day planned, with errands, lunch at a favorite restaurant, and a duck pond visit. I held her hand and simply asked God for the rain to end soon if that was okay with Him. The rain continued while we dressed and ate breakfast. But when we stepped outside and opened the umbrella, the clouds shifted to reveal the sun, and the rain stopped. I closed the umbrella and expressed my surprise. Sadie said, "Well, we asked God for that." She could have said, "What did you expect?" Little Sadie reminded me that God can do anything, and if I make a request, I should anticipate a response.

—Becky

God, I want an expectant faith like that! Amen.

attention

Give ear, O Lord, unto my prayer; and attend to the
voice of my supplications.
—Psalm 86:6 KJV

My husband, Steve, and I were walking in the park when I noticed a tiny dog, part Chihuahua and part Yorkie, walking with an elderly owner. "What a cute dog!" I said, and the owner stopped. As I paid attention to the dog, she talked about what a great companion Sophie had been since her husband died of cancer the year before. In the span of five minutes she fondly remembered her husband, a veteran and a Sunday school teacher for twenty-five years. Then she said, "Will you pray for me?" So right there in the middle of the park, my husband and I prayed with a stranger. Our initial connection was based on her dog catching my eye, but God was calling attention to something far greater—the heart of a lonely, grieving widow.

—Penne

Thank You, God, for always hearing the cries of our hearts.
Amen.

confident

Stand up straight and realize who you are,
that you tower over your circumstances. You are
a child of God. Stand up straight.
—Maya Angelou

I first learned to pray in my kindergarten Sunday-school class. Seated at a miniature table in chairs painted in gaudy colors, we bowed our heads and closed our eyes. Three decades later, I was shocked when friends at a Bible study told me, "Hold up your head when you talk to God. You are His child. You have every right to come to Him and ask for what you need and want." What a radical idea! Then I thought of my own kids. I didn't want them to hang their heads when they asked me for a favor, but rather to look up confidently, believing that I love them and will freely share everything I have.

—Jeanette

*Dear Lord, help me remember that although
You are God, You are also my Father. Amen.*

groanings

Now in the same way the Spirit also helps
our weakness; for we do not know what to pray for
as we should, but the Spirit Himself intercedes
for us with groanings too deep for words.
—Romans 8:26 NASB

had a season in my life when I felt I was in a fight with God.
I didn't want to make necessary changes. I dug in. I didn't
know how to pray. I grumbled a lot, and I groaned. When I
read the verse above and discovered that the Holy Spirit was so
invested in me that He intercedes and advocates for me with
"groanings," I was both humbled and contrite.

Deep prayer is tough, but it's great to know that as I was
groaning all those years, the Holy Spirit was groaning, too,
interceding faithfully for me. I wasn't fighting against God.
Rather, He was fighting victoriously for me.

—Carol

*Holy Spirit, You are my warrior God who battles
for me with deep groanings. Amen.*

soon

The God of peace will soon crush Satan under your feet.
—Romans 16:20 NIV

When I was a child, my parents used two words that I came to hate: *maybe* and *soon*. The first, I learned, really meant no. And "soon" never seemed to come soon enough.

Paul, the great first-century church-planter and letter-writer, wrote to followers of Jesus who were enduring a season of severe tribulation, "The God of peace will soon crush Satan under your feet. The grace of our Lord Jesus be with you" (Rom. 16:20 NIV). The word *soon* was intended to give them comfort and hope in difficult circumstances. If you're in a trying season, pray "soon" as often as you can. Pray it as a request: "Soon, please." Pray it as an affirmation: "Soon, I believe." Pray it as a reminder: "Remember: soon."

—Bob

Father, let my "soon" come in Your perfect and gracious timing.
Amen.

mind

Do not conform to the pattern of this world, but be
transformed by the renewing of your mind. Then you will
be able to test and approve what God's will is—his good,
pleasing and perfect will.
—Romans 12:2 NIV

My mind often feels scattered. Information overload.
Work pressures. Family dynamics. Ministry commitments. The worries and unknowns of life often
short-circuit my brain. *How can I figure out God's will when
I can't even navigate my day?* I need a mind transformation.
I need my neurons to fire in a different way. God's presence
and words of truth rewire how I see things, changing priorities,
bringing peace in the midst of chaos, resetting my moods with
His grace. I want my mind to be transformed by His love so I
can walk out my days in His good, pleasing, and perfect will.
—Susanna

*God, renew my mind. Help me to think, observe, and process as
You do so I can navigate this incredible life You have given me.
Amen.*

revive

Your promise revives me; it comforts me in all my troubles.
—Psalm 119:50 NLT

A sprout of green broke through the soil. "My calla lily is coming back!" I poked my husband and pointed to the spot in my flower bed that had lain barren last season with no sign of life from the elegant, exotic flower that had bloomed there for years. I was certain my calla was dead. But as this new spring turned to summer, the lily blossomed as gracefully as ever, revived perhaps by heavy spring rains or maybe from a season of rest. I understand the calla lily. Sometimes my soul needs to be nourished or my body needs rest so I can bloom again. Sometimes an old dream or a dormant friendship needs to be revived. As I admire the new lily, I'm thankful for how God continues to revive me.

—Karen

Father, in You I am miraculously revived into something new and beautiful. Amen.

meditation

May my meditation be pleasing to him, as I rejoice in the LORD.
—Psalm 104:34 NIV

Y ou could talk about meditation at a fancy New York cocktail party and others would leap in and exclaim, "I do it too!" It's almost become a fad. But meditation is part of my Christian prayer practice. Meditation and God? Yes, the two go hand in hand—in fact, the words *meditate* or *meditation* appear countless times in the Bible, mostly in the Psalms. So, I'm encouraged to meditate on God's Word, meditate on Scripture, meditate on the power of God in my life. When I meditate, I close my eyes, pay attention to my worries, hearing them. Then I give my concerns over to God and let them go, rejoicing.

—Rick

Dear Lord, thank You for biblical meditation, an avenue to seek You and find You. Let the "words of my mouth and the meditation of my heart be acceptable in Your sight" (Ps. 19:14). Amen.

provide

What a serene and quiet life might you lead if you would
leave providing to the God of providence!
—Charles Haddon Spurgeon

Newly married, living in one room, attending seminary on
a spartan budget, our schedules left my wife and me
no means of increasing our income. We did our best to
scrape by, but often cried out to God in our helplessness. Each
time, the mail soon brought a welcome windfall from a family
member or friend.

Those moments taught us to remember God's provision
in the past and ask in faith for His provision in the future—just
as Barnabas and Paul reminded the people of Lystra that God
"has shown kindness by giving you rain from heaven and crops
in their seasons; he provides you with plenty of food and fills
your hearts with joy" (Acts 14:17 NIV). To this day, I often repeat
a one-word prayer—"provide"—so I remember to call on God's
faithfulness and generosity.

—Bob

Lord, remind me often: You will provide. Amen.

money

But store up for yourselves treasures in heaven.
—Matthew 6:20 NIV

I hope I don't sound pretentious, but I was born into a very affluent family. It's only taken me six decades of life to realize it. Growing up, other girls seemed to have much more than I did. If I wanted something pretty to wear, I might have to reimagine a castoff curtain into a new frock. And all of this happened against the backdrop of a mother who strung half-runner beans on the porch and sang, "O, How I Love Jesus." Her focus was never on this earth's treasures but on a faraway place called heaven. Sometimes Mom's thinking seemed hopelessly outdated. But she passed on a spiritual wealth that has seen me through every struggle. Turns out, I haven't needed much else.

—Roberta

Thank You, Lord, for mothers who teach us the ways of Your riches. Amen.

water

Whoever drinks the water I give them will never thirst. Indeed,
the water I give them will become in them a spring of
water welling up to eternal life.
—John 4:14 NIV

I don't drink enough water. I set out to drink the recom-
mended amount, but I fall short. I usually try to catch up on
water right before bedtime, and you know what that means…
Why do I do that? I love the taste of water. I live in superhot
Florida. I run, sweat, and get thirsty. Drinking lots of water
makes me feel good and makes my skin look better. What's my
problem? I guess it's just another case of not doing what I want
to do (Rom. 7:15). I admit it's sometimes that way with Jesus
too. I know He has water that will quench my thirst, but when I
look for other thirst-quenchers, I miss out on the lasting, living
water that satisfies for eternity.

—Isabella

Dear Jesus, help me thirst for You, the Living Water! Amen.

tabernacle

Then a cloud covered the tent of the congregation, and the
glory of the LORD filled the tabernacle.
—Exodus 40:34 KJV

A few months ago, I drove down to be with my adult daughter, Emerald, to nurse her back to health after she'd had surgery. My daughter also asked my sister to come down and be her personal chef for the six weeks of recovery. Before Penne got there, I did all the cooking, cleaning, and all the errands. I was grateful when help arrived.

Early in the stillness of each morning, my sister and I shared our devotional time together on the balcony. We had comfortable furniture, a table for our Bibles and books, plugs for our music, and outdoor carpet for our bare feet. The weather was incredibly pleasant, and a hummingbird visited us every day. As we communed with God morning after morning, the balcony became our tabernacle of praise.

—Rosalind

God, thank You for Your glory each day. Amen.

acceptance

God grant me the serenity to accept the things
I cannot change.
—Serenity Prayer

'm stubborn. That's no secret. I like to have control when it comes to things about myself. And with that stubbornness comes refusal to accept. I find it hard to give up things that are way beyond my control. If I just try a little harder, why can't I change things? But as I've been told and as I have seen, there are some things that simply cannot be changed. I have to learn to accept things as they are and not how I want them to be. I have to let go of the frustration that rises when I can't make things go the way I want or need them to. Let it go. There's no use dwelling on something you have no chance of changing. Acceptance isn't always easy, but I strive toward it every day.

—Sabrina

*Please, Lord, give me the patience to accept the things
that are out of my control. Amen.*

lead

Lead us not into temptation.
—Matthew 6:13 NIV

O n our first trip to the Holy Land, my wife and I checked into our hotel after dark. In the morning we were delighted to open the curtains and see on the hillside below a young man leading a small herd of sheep along a narrow path. We watched as the shepherd set the pace, scanned the way ahead for dangers and obstacles, and checked behind him every so often to make sure his charges stayed on the right path.

Those who pray the Lord's Prayer ask God to "lead us," though most rush right into the next phrase: "not into temptation." But before moving on in prayer, I like to insert a pause between the phrases so I first ask God to set the pace, watch for and warn of dangers and obstacles, and make sure I stay on the right path—all expressed in the single word: "Lead."

—Bob

Savior, like a shepherd, lead me. Amen.

tweak

*While they were saying among themselves
it cannot be done, it was done.*
—Helen Keller

A tweak here, a tweak there, a tweak everywhere. Being born without a left arm, most tasks require me to make an adjustment of some kind. I taught myself to type with one hand. I reached for every key from a "home row" as instructed in Typing 101, but did it all with my right hand. I used my prosthetic left hand to hold down the shift key, as needed. Without the sense of touch, sometimes I accidentally pressed a key above or below it. A simple tweak solved the problem—I covered the shift key with two layers of Velcro. It raised the touch point just enough for me to always hit the right key.

Today may bring a new challenge, but with God's help, I can figure out a tweak, apply it, and keep moving forward.

—Becky

Thank You, God, for my difficult, wonderful life. Amen.

extravagant

I'll make a list of God's gracious dealings...his great
goodness...compassion lavished, love extravagant.
—Isaiah 63:7–8 MSG

Around Easter, Jewish families celebrate Passover, when the angel of death passed over the homes of Jewish slaves in Egypt, sparing their children. For two nights, at a dinner called a *seder*, this story is recounted in Scripture and songs. My favorite song is "Dayenu," which means "it would have been enough" in Hebrew, and lists miracles from God. Here are a few lines: *If He had split the sea for us, and had not taken us through it on dry land, it would have been enough! If he had taken us through the sea on dry land and had not drowned our oppressors in it, it would have been enough!*

The last line says that while any miracle would have been enough, God did all those miracles for His children. *That's* extravagant love.

—Michelle

*Father, I'm so glad You love me extravagantly.
Help me to love others that way too. Amen.*

surprise

Expect nothing. Live frugally on surprise.
—Alice Walker

Neither my mom nor sister can keep a secret, but I can, which means *I* get to surprise them. For my sister's birthday one year I had a T-shirt made featuring a funny photo from our early childhood. Last year after army training, I made a surprise trip home for Mother's Day. I also ordered my mom a brand of crackers she discovered in a New York City store during her last visit. She loved the crackers but couldn't find them in her town. After I'd placed the order, I was surprised to find that the email confirmation didn't have an estimated shipping date. Had I placed the order too late? Or maybe too early? A couple days before the holiday, she called—an interesting package had arrived. Right on time.

—Allison

Lord, it's no surprise You love us. Help me continue to share that love with those around me. Amen.

gratitude

As we express our gratitude, we must never
forget that the highest appreciation is not
to utter words, but to live by them.
—John F. Kennedy

Entering my kitchen today, I smile. The counter is crowded with love. Remnants of a dessert left from a party sit beside a plate of baklava, a carrot cake, and a batch of cookies, all presented to us by different friends. Our vegetable bin overflows with the bounty of another dear one's garden. My kitchen—and my heart—are full. As I pause to think of ways to show my gratitude, a few ideas come to mind.

When I consider all Jesus has done and continues to do for me, I'm overwhelmed. I can never repay the grace He's given me. The gift of eternity. It's impossible.

But as I live mindful of those blessings, I can offer Him a spirit filled with gratitude, and pay them forward.

—Heidi

*Lord, let me show my gratitude, not only with words,
but with my life. Amen.*

ebenezer

Here I raise my Ebenezer, Hither by Thy help I've come.
—from the hymn "Come Thou Fount of Every Blessing,"
written by Robert Robinson

My wife and I faced a huge life change in our early sixties when she changed jobs and we moved across the country to an area we'd never lived in before. So much about the transition was not only unfamiliar but also hard. When one of us began to get overwhelmed, the other would sometimes offer a reminder that God had led us safely thus far and was still guiding our steps.

When ancient Israel won a key battle against their enemies, "Samuel took a stone and set it up between Mizpah and Shen. He named it Ebenezer, saying, 'Thus far the LORD has helped us'" (1 Sam. 7:12 NIV). My wife and I are gratefully settled now, but we still occasionally pray "Ebenezer" for ourselves or others, remembering and calling on God's faithfulness to date—and beyond.

—Bob

I raise an "Ebenezer" today. Help us, Lord. Amen.

teamwork

Then they came to Him, bringing a paralytic
who was carried by four men.
—Mark 2:3 NKJV

People gathered in Spain for a global, quadrennial sporting event. I was a spectator and part of a global mission group. Following an outdoor, dramatic gospel presentation, I approached a local Spanish gentleman who was interested in hearing more about the skit's message. Noticing the language barrier, a man from Canada sought a translator. He first enlisted a lady from South Africa who spoke French (the gentleman's second language) and then a lady from Mexico, fluent in Spanish. Our impromptu, improbable team of four (American, Canadian, South African, Mexican) together explained the skit's message to our new Spanish friend. He embraced the gospel and thanked us, grateful for the message that was timely for him as a husband and father-to-be. As the saying goes, "Teamwork makes the dream work."

—Steve

*Thank You, Lord, for guiding us to work with others
on Your team. Amen.*

breathe

Breathe in deeply to bring your mind home to your body.
—Thich Nhat

I n times of stress and anxiety I often find myself forgetting to do one thing: breathe. I'll be so concerned over the little, big, or everything-in-between things that I forget to take a moment for myself. When that deep pain in my chest starts to rise, for a moment I pause in confusion. *What's going on? Why am I feeling this way?* The answer is simple. I didn't take a breath. I'd let anxiety and stress take over.

When the world feels as if it's resting on my shoulders and nothing is going the way I planned, I have to remember that stopping and taking a long, deep breath is what centers me. I have to regroup and tell myself everything will be okay. Step back. Breathe. Inhale and exhale. Then I feel better.

—Sabrina

Thank You, God, for reminding me in times of stress to just take a moment and breathe. Amen.

beyond

Now all glory to God, who is able, through his mighty power at work within us, to accomplish infinitely more than we might ask or think.
—Ephesians 3:20 NLT

I f my cats had peeked into the future on adoption day, they would've high-fived their shelter mates. The word *spoil* can't begin to describe how I baby them. Two flavors of food. Treats for simply looking cute. And nicknames I'm embarrassed to tell you. A few days ago I opened the back door at dusk and in my best Minnie Mouse voice, I called my furry children, "Come inside so I can give you treats. I love to give to my babies!" Immediately I thought of God's enormous heart. How He enjoys lavishing His children with blessings. Guidance for the path ahead. Comfort in our loneliness. Healing. Strength. Eternal life. Not spoiling. But always going above and beyond.

—Jeanette

Dear God, thank You for giving us all of You.
Please let me reflect Your generous heart. Amen.

thanks

Give thanks to the LORD, for he is good.
—1 Chronicles 16:34 NIV

---

often start my day reluctantly. Sluggish. Groggy. Grumpy. So much changes, however, when I turn to my daily habit of saying thanks. Thanks for a good night's sleep. Thanks for a bed and a pillow. Thanks for hot water. For indoor plumbing (ever lived without it?). For toothpaste. For soap. Thanks for a roof over my head, clothes to wear, food to eat, and coffee to drink, hallelujah, amen!

That short and simple word—*thanks*—can set (or change) the tone of your whole day. Try it. Start your day with it, and punctuate your day with it. See how many things—including diverse things—you can say "thanks" for today.

—Bob

God, thank You for this day and for the many good reasons I have to say "thanks." Amen.

heart

Blessed are the pure in heart, for they shall see God.
—Matthew 5:8 ESV

'm an easy-to-approach and very empathetic person. Seeing people happy or sad can elicit deep emotion in me. Sometimes it's almost as if I can literally feel what others feel. See into their hearts. Those feelings can overwhelm me. But I've decided to view things differently and consider my empathy as one of my personal strengths. I often get compliments on how well I handle conflicts and situations. Friends and family come to me for advice or support. Being able to empathize with people makes me more open to helping others and giving them a chance to feel comfortable with me and see my heart as someone who cares, and cares deeply.

—Jaylin

Lord, thank You for giving me an open and caring heart and a love of helping other people. Amen.

diligently

But without faith it is impossible to please him: for he that
cometh to God must believe that he is, and that he is a
rewarder of them that diligently seek him.
—Hebrews 11:6 KJV

O ver the past two years, a young woman I know named
Stephanie went from being a curious participant in
my small-group Bible study, to leading her own small-
group Bible study, to preaching her first sermon! Stephanie
was working as a respiratory therapist until God nudged her to
pursue a master's in biblical studies. At first, she was nervous
about going back to school full-time. How would she cover all
the expenses? But again, she diligently sought God for direction and did whatever He said. Relying on faith she left her job.
Then a group of people who were inspired by Stephanie's dili-
gence gave her all the money she needed. God always rewards
those who diligently seek Him.

—Penne

Dear Lord, help me to diligently seek You in all that I do. Amen.

wander

Prone to wander, Lord, I feel it, prone to leave
the God I love; take my heart, O take and seal it,
seal it for Thy courts above.
—from the hymn "Come Thou Fount of Every
Blessing," by Robert Robinson

As a small child, I had the propensity to wander. One minute I was in the grocery store with my mom, the next I was alone in the candy aisle, distracted by chocolate. *Did she leave me?* I spent several heart-pounding moments searching until I found her. With tears of relief, I would lean into her side. I was safe.

This pattern often mirrors my spiritual life. I wander. I am pulled by my heart's selfish desires, pride, or control issues. Instead of remaining near my Heavenly Father, I wander into anxiousness or anger or depression. *Did He leave me?* Nope. He remains steady and faithful, ready to take me back into His loving arms. Finding my way back to Him, I am safe.

—Susanna

Father, keep me from wandering and help me to lean into You.
Amen.

offering

Jesus said, "Truly I tell you, this poor widow has put more into the treasury than all the others. They all gave out of their wealth; but she, out of her poverty, put in everything—all she had to live on."
—Mark 12:43–44 NIV

A small crowd had gathered to listen to several musicians playing soothing music in the midst of Grand Central Station, one of New York City's busiest thoroughfares. People were dropping dollars of varying amounts into a container in front of the quartet. I dropped in a dollar. Then a lady who appeared to be homeless walked forward, bent down solemnly, and gently placed the newspaper she was holding next to the collection box. The Scripture above came to mind, and I wondered, *Did anyone else see what I just saw?* For a brief moment, the cavernous lobby of Grand Central became a sanctuary as a lady gave all she had, a sacred offering.

—Janet

Lord, help me to give everything I have. Amen.

old

The great thing about getting older is that
you don't lose all the other ages you've been.
—Madeleine L'Engle

The oldest thing in my house is a stuffed dog named Marbles. He was an unintentional hand-me-down from my older brother. When I found him in a linen closet, I was four. Marbles was twelve, the same age as my brother. Marbles was well worn. His nose was rubbed off, both ears torn; he was even bald in a few spots. He was old, but I threw him a birthday party. (His cake had four candles, like mine.) Since then, Marbles and I have gone to college, traveled abroad, and moved to New York City, where we live now. After all our years together, I'm showing signs of wear myself. I know Marbles understands.

—Meg

*Lord, help me appreciate each day I'm given,
no matter how old I am. Amen.*

new

Behold, I make all things new.
—Revelation 21:5 KJV

Five years old, Christmas morning, and all I could think about was that new coat. One just like my television cowboy hero, Kid Curry, wore. I still remember the feeling, the green gift wrap falling away, and there it was. I shrugged it on, my excitement so intense I thought I'd explode with happiness on the spot.

Funny, I don't know whatever happened to that coat. Along with my high-riding hero, Kid Curry, its novelty eventually faded like gun smoke on the high-noon breeze. Then again, earthly "new" always fades, doesn't it?

But don't touch that dial. There is an *unearthly* Hero who never fades. In fact, His mercy is new every morning. New only becomes *newer*. Just look back—the trail is practically littered with green paper.

And the very best part? The ride is just getting started.

—Buck

Lord, You are a constant and wonderful surprise. I will follow You all of my days. You make all things new! Amen.

bewildered

I weren't never lost, but I was bewildered a time or two.
—Daniel Boone

At the end of his long life, famed frontiersman Daniel Boone was asked by a reporter if he'd ever been lost in the wilderness. Boone shook his head no. "I weren't never lost," he replied. "But I was bewildered a time or two."

As a fan of history and folklore, I love this story. I live near the Cumberland Gap where, in 1775, Boone led some of the earliest American pioneers west across the Appalachian Mountains into what would become Kentucky and Tennessee. He was brave, strong, and true. Another reason I love the quote? Boone refused to use the word *lost*, which often implies defeat. Better to choose a more optimistic word.

Whenever I struggle to find my way in times that are some-times dark and confusing, I remember that I'm not really lost. I'm just bewildered.

—Jennie

*Remind me, Lord, that with You beside me I'm never truly lost.
Amen.*

statutes

You are good and You do good; teach me Your statutes.
—Psalm 119:68 NASB

always wanted to be a good parent—but the parenting journey was challenging. I realized early on that I needed to look outside myself for help. I looked to my parents and they gave great advice. Then I looked to my Heavenly Father, and He pointed me to the pages of ancient wisdom in the Psalms, Proverbs, and Paul's epistles. Sure enough, God's statutes have helped me and my husband to be better parents. I can see the effects in our daughter's life. She is strong, responsible, and on her own journey to know God. Some view God's statutes negatively. I find His rules to be relevant for my needs today. The most important statute that I've embraced is, "Train up a child in the way he should go, and when he is old, he will not depart from it" (Prov. 22:6 NKJV).

—Rosalind

Lord, help me to keep Your statutes. Amen.

sustenance

And the angel of the LORD came again the second time, and touched him, and said, Arise and eat; because the journey is too great for thee.
—1 Kings 19:7 KJV

Sometimes I'm too busy to eat, and I know I'm not alone. In 1 Kings 19, the prophet Elijah is on the run from Jezebel. He's so exhausted both physically and mentally he loses perspective (1 Kings 19:4). Worn out, Elijah falls asleep under a tree. An angel wakes him up saying, "Arise and eat," and points to water and hot food lying beside him. Elijah conks out again, and once more the angel awakens him, urging him to eat so he can endure his journey. That food sustains him for forty days!

As much as I need food and water, I also need Jesus's daily Bread and living Water, which is life-giving sustenance in the form of daily Scripture and fellowshipping with Him. Strength for my journey.

—Janet

Lord, thank You for sustaining me day by day. Amen.

consider

Only fear the LORD, and serve him in truth with all your heart:
for consider how great things he hath done for you.
—1 Samuel 12:24 KJV

Has any generation been as busy as ours? As a child, I was always observing and considering the world around me, drawing conclusions about it and my place in it through careful thought. As an adult, in this busy era, I often feel as if thinking too much is at best the enemy of much-needed efficiency.

But Scripture invites me to consider: "Consider the lilies," Jesus said. Who among us would look at a lily and see the promise of God's provision? To *consider* opens me to different possibilities, new layers of meaning and appreciation, deeper understandings.

Today, as I go about my busy day, I want to stop, even for a moment, and consider what something unassuming like a lily might teach me.

—Jon

Lord, help me stop to consider all You have done for me. Amen.

quality

The quality of a person's life is in direct proportion to their commitment to excellence.
—Vince Lombardi

I wish I could visit with you over a cup at my favorite coffee shop on roasting day. A rich, woodsy scent permeates the air as the owner sits on a stool beside the coffee-bean roaster with a stopwatch and a clipboard. He watches a digital display and records the rise in temperature over time. He listens carefully for the "first crack" of the beans. His nuanced sense of smell determines when the beans have achieved the perfect aroma and are ready to be brewed and served. I wonder if I approach my passions with a similar commitment to excellence and a desire to produce something of the very best quality. Are my senses attuned to God so I can align with His timing, hear His direction, and serve Him with my very best?

—Karen

Father, thank You for blessing my life with quality when I commit to Your excellence. Amen.

yadah

I will praise the name of God with a song,
and will magnify him with thanksgiving.
—Psalms 69:30 KJV

When I moved to Savannah, I wondered if I would find friends like the friends I left behind in my little college town. Within a year and a half, I met three women, Tonya, Valarie, and Lisa, who added so much value to my life. We four knew our friendship was a God appointment. In fact, it was so special we named ourselves the "Yadah Sisters." *Yadah* in Hebrew means praise, and we decided we would praise the name of God regardless of our circumstances. Since then, we have laughed, cried, prayed, and praised together. One day we drove miles to enjoy a beautiful sunrise on the beach. We had an unforgettable experience beholding the beauty of God in nature. On that faithful morning, we joined with all creation in songs of praise to our God.

—Penne

Lord, today we praise Your name with a song. Amen.

adapt

If we fail to adapt, we fail to move forward.
—John Wooden

'm not someone who needs variety in his life. For breakfast I eat a bowl of oatmeal. Every day. For lunch I have a turkey sandwich and ten baby carrots. Always. But change is required in today's world. Learning, growing is all about being able to adapt. In such times I'm reminded of when my parents came to visit from out of state. I'd planned a fancy meal with roast turkey. But when it came time to put the bird in the oven, I discovered my mother had pies baking. It seemed a disaster in the making. Until I remembered the grill. I had no choice but to adapt. The turkey turned out perfect. So well that, I cook it on the grill every time now. God is always present and helps me adapt. That's the one thing I know I can count on.

—Evan

Lord, help me to remember I don't have to adapt on my own.
Amen.

obedience

Does it make sense to pray for guidance about the future
if we are not obeying in the thing that lies before us today?
How many momentous events in Scripture depended on
one person's seemingly small act of obedience!
—Elisabeth Elliot

It's hardly a popular concept. Obedience. Yet there's a clue to what it's about in the very root of the word. *Obedience* is literally "to listen to," from the Latin *ob*, "to," and *audire*, "listen" or "hear." No wonder it's one of the monastic virtues, listening and obeying God. In Bible stories I've found compelling examples of obedience. Abraham left his homeland, Paul preached the gospel, Mary became the Mother of God, Jesus died on the cross. They listened and heard. I aspire to do the same.

—Rick

Lord, help me see the ways You are calling me, ways that I might never have expected. Let me say yes and obey Your call with joy and humility. Amen.

mine

Fear not, for I have redeemed you; I have called you by
your name; You are Mine.
—Isaiah 43:1 NKJV

Last week, my daughter and I spent an afternoon shopping together in a large department store. In addition to being petite, we both have different interests, so it didn't take long for us to lose sight of each other. I'd forgotten my phone, so when I spotted the top of her head above a clothing rack, I called out her name. She turned her head in my direction, a look of relief spread across her face. Her expression reminded me of when she was a child.

Years ago, when I was lost, God called me to Him. I welcomed the sense of security I experienced when I turned to Him. I will never again slip out of sight of my Father. But if I wander off, I know He'll call me back where I belong.

—Heidi

Lord, thank You for claiming me as Yours. Amen.

cleanse

Let us draw near to God with a sincere heart and with the full assurance that faith brings, having our hearts sprinkled to cleanse us from a guilty conscience.
—Hebrews 10:22 NIV

G rowing up, a friend and I would often spend a Sunday afternoon (between morning and evening church services) playing in the woods near my home. Upon our return, my mother would shake her head, amazed. Somehow, my friend would look as clean and buttoned-down as when we left the house, but I would be covered in dirt, mud, and virtually every impurity the woods had to offer, necessitating a thorough scrubbing before Mom pronounced me fit for public viewing.

I don't play as much in the woods as I used to, but I am prone to wander and wallow in the dust and dirt of daily life, so I draw near to God for daily confession and cleansing from all guilt and shame.

—Bob

Lord, cleanse me today of all the dust and dirt of daily life. Amen.

transform

Program your mind with what God says about you and a
transformation will take place.
—Joel Osteen

When I got married, I gained seventy pounds. After Pierce was born three years in, I got motivated to lose that weight. I joined Weight Watchers. I walked on a treadmill. Over time, I started running, eventually as much as seven miles a day. I added resistance training to build strength. It took time, willingness, and patience, but now my body is transformed and I'm more fit than when I was thirty.

God is much more efficient. He has transformed me from death to life, with virtually no effort on my part other than willingness, sometimes desperate willingness. In fact, the most striking changes in my character and habits have surprised me, sudden deliverance through grace alone. I believe this is the reality of my Christian journey and the heart of the quote above.

—Isabella

*Lord, help me willingly allow You to transform me
into the person You intend me to be. Amen.*

joyfulness

Consider it pure joy, my brothers and sisters, whenever you face trials of many kinds, because you know that the testing of your faith produces perseverance.
—James 1:2–3 NIV

A few years ago, I got cancer and stopped working. Six months later, my husband, Carlos, got laid off, leaving us both without health insurance. With few options, we eventually secured health insurance, but it was costly—and my oncologist didn't accept it. Our savings dwindled, and I wasn't getting any better, but Carlos and I are prayer warriors. We've witnessed God's miracles. So after placing our situation in God's hands, we started to cry out with joy, refusing to complain. Yes, we'd hit rock bottom, but no one could tell, because we saturated our lives with joy and laughter.

—Didi

Father, thank You for drawing me closer to You in every experience. You are my joy! Amen.

fruit

Bearing fruit in every good work.
—Colossians 1:10 NASB

Years ago I bought a postcard with a painting of a pear tree bending its fruit—a perfect golden pear—to a girl standing on tiptoe. I'm a fruit lover. When our youngest was in kindergarten, she and I would sit in the backyard sun after school and eat juicy pears. Maybe that's why the postcard caught my eye. But more than that, I was attracted to the tree offering its fruit. Making an effort. Placing it within reach. God's Word says followers of Christ are fruit bearers—the kind who make an effort to place His love and loyalty, His kindness and forgiveness, His peace and joy within reach of others. Flavorful fruit for all to savor.

—Carol

Your fruit, Lord, is meant to be shared freely and abundantly. Amen.

balance

Seek patience and passion in equal amounts.
Patience alone will not build the temple. Passion alone
will destroy its walls.
—Maya Angelou

Earlier this year I experienced a vague sense of melancholy several times. *What's wrong with me, Lord?* God's whisper flew into my heart swift as an arrow. "You're too busy. Working too hard. Expecting yourself to be Jesus Jr." I smiled at that preposterous thought. But I had to agree. Often I slip into the erroneous belief that the universe will stop if I rest or play. God's joking comment reminded me that I need times of recreation to balance the hours of work. Now, I refuse to let false guilt condemn me when I watch a comedy show with my family, or read a novel with a bowl of popcorn in my lap. God didn't create me to be a human doing, but a human being.

—Jeanette

Lord, give me wisdom to find balance between work and play,
between passion and patience, between achieving and resting.
Amen.

simplify

Our life is frittered away by detail...Simplify. Simplify. Simplify.
—Henry David Thoreau

I try not to spend money on things I don't need. I value the simple life, but I can find myself being seduced by the latest gadget. When it seems as if everyone I know has a smart speaker that plays music with a voice command, I get to thinking I need one too. My children face worse peer pressure than I do. But my favorite family memories are the times when we did without. Like the time when my son's video game player died, and we spent an afternoon building a log cabin out of Popsicle sticks. Or when our dishwasher broke and doing dishes by hand turned into a great family bonding time. Not surprisingly, those are the times I've felt closest to God, too. No app required. It's simple.

—Evan

Lord, help me to simplify life's choices by putting You first. Amen.

plans

Many are the plans in a person's heart, but it is the LORD's
purpose that prevails.
—Proverbs 19:21 NIV

After college, my plan was to get an apartment and a great teaching fellowship. But then I didn't get accepted. Without the fellowship, I felt like a failure, lost, rejected, and confused. My worth was deeply rooted in being validated by my family, but I finally realized that my priorities were in the wrong place. It started to dawn on me that the teaching fellowship had been *my* plan for me, but maybe not God's plan for me, so I went on with my life. But God never forgot about my heart's desire. His purpose for me to teach is being fulfilled right now…and my little students bring me so much joy!

—Kiana

*Dear Father, thank You that Your plans are
always greater than my plans. Amen.*

adventure

Adventure is not outside man, it's within.
—George Eliot

Adventure is my thing! I've skydived. Jumped into a pool of ice water. I've even attempted to eat a raw clam (hey, that was challenging for me). Most people would say I'm daring, but I haven't always been.

Years ago, on a corporate team-building trip, I recall standing on a ledge several feet above the ground with my back to my colleagues who were waiting below. They were nudging me to trust them and fall into their arms, a new adventure for me. I heard their encouraging voices, but I couldn't see if they were *really* ready to catch me. I feared they would drop me. I hesitated for a long time, but eventually I decided to let go of my fears, trust, and fall backward. They caught me…just as God always does.

—Ty'Ann

Lord, thank You for being with me in all my adventures.

flower

Where flowers bloom, so does hope.
—Lady Bird Johnson

My mom is an expert gardener. My dad, her right-hand man, accomplishes her botanical visions. Last year they loaded a water-filled kiddie pool into the back of their rental car just so they could transport three hydrangea bushes. They drove over seven hundred miles to plant them in my front yard! Hydrangeas, with their clustered blooms, are my favorite flower. I panicked this winter when the blossoms shriveled on the stem. I called my mom and she reassured me, "Don't worry. They'll come back." She was right. They came back with a vengeance. Flower upon flower, full of life and hope. God often allows new growth to flower in my life after a dark season. He resurrects dreams, ushers in mercy, and breathes life into desperate moments with His undeniable love. The flower of hope is the most beautiful of all.

—Susanna

God, allow Your hope to flower in my heart, putting down deep roots, showing off Your beautiful love. Amen.

connect

I can do things you cannot, you can do things I cannot;
together we can do great things.
—Mother Teresa

Knowing that there are so many people with experiences wildly different from mine, I always look for a way to form meaningful connections with those around me. Connecting with other people can provide new knowledge and understanding. I've always considered myself a people person, and am happy to be a friend to all, or a listening ear when someone's in need. Although challenging sometimes, it's also beneficial for me to open up to others. As I connect with others and share views and experiences, I'm learning that together we can create wonderful things now and in the future.

—Jaylin

Lord, challenge me to reach out, open up, and connect with new people, to share my knowledge and learn from theirs. Amen.

between

Now faith is the substance of things hoped for,
the evidence of things not seen.
—Hebrews 11:1 NKJV

As I write this, I'm in between jobs. Actually, I'm between
life chapters, with assorted big things in transition. I
don't like it. I don't like the in-between places of life
when I don't know what comes next. I like a plan, preferably
detailed and according to my specifications. God seldom
seems to work that way for me. Seems like He expects me to
have faith! He might even give me a vision of where He's taking
me, but then just leaves me hanging. As though He's reminding
me to rest in His complete reliability and competence to exe-
cute a good plan on my behalf—perhaps one that will surprise,
delight, challenge, and grow me up in Him.

—Isabella

*God, help me trust Your good plan and enjoy the in-between
times in faith. Amen.*

build

We have come to know and believe the love
God has for us. God is love.
—1 John 4:16 NLV

I watched my two neighbors building a fence. One was six feet tall or so, the other less than half that. The tall one had a tool belt and a metal hammer. The shorter, a matching belt with a plastic hammer. Father and son, working side by side. I watched the little guy pound away at those boards. Dad just smiled.

How many times have I set out to accomplish some great work for God, telling myself all the while that I actually have something to bring to the table? And He, in His grace, hands me a plastic hammer and invites me to give it my best.

In the end, I shake my head. "Lord, I didn't bring anything to this at all."

He takes me into His arms. "You brought *you*. And that's all I've ever wanted."

—Buck

Thank You, Lord. You are the Good Father! Amen.

prosper

"For I know the plans I have for you," declares the LORD,
"plans to prosper you and not to harm you, plans to give
you a hope and a future."
—Jeremiah 29:11 NIV

When the Israelites were taken into captivity in Babylon, God told them they wouldn't always be stuck in a foreign land: He had plans for them to prosper! The Hebrew word for *prosper* means "to push forward, to pass through, to get on." God was going to move His children through their current circumstances and on to a better place—to where they belonged.

This is a promise that I can—and should—always claim. God has plans for me. Good plans for me to prosper! Will God send me a windfall of money? Probably not. But He does better than that: He pushes me forward through present concerns to a place where I can rest in Him.

—Michelle

Lord, thank You for Your plans to prosper me; help me to always rely on Your guidance. Amen.

amazing

Yes, the LORD has done amazing things for us! What joy!
—Psalm 126:3 NLT

'm known for saying such things as "That restaurant has amazing food." "You look amazing!" "It was an amazing experience." *Amazing* is a word that I often overuse to indicate top-notch, great, or impressive.

But there are so many other things that are truly awe-inspiring that I often take for granted. I woke up this morning. The cut I had on my finger twenty-four hours ago is nearly gone today. I can hear and enjoy the birds chirping away outside. I can see the flowers that were tight blossoms yesterday have now bloomed. The sun shines in a cloudless sky. Amazing comes in the small, overlooked stuff of everyday life. Great or small, God has done amazing things for us.

—Barbranda

Lord, open my eyes to the great things You do every day.
In Jesus's name. Amen.

compassion

We can't heal the world today, but we can begin with a
voice of compassion, a heart of love, an act of kindness.
—Mary Davis

Someone shoots me an email, calls, or nabs me after
church. "Would you please say a prayer for me…" Or I
hear of a worrisome event, an illness, a job loss, a marriage in trouble, an upcoming diagnosis. "I'll pray for you,"
I say, or I use my father's phrase, "I'll hold a good thought."
Either way, I like to say the prayer right then and there. While I
remember. What I've come to see is that the compassion I feel,
the outpouring of my concern, the email I send, or the listening
I do *is* an important part of the prayer. Just like my dad put it:
"I'll hold a good thought."

—Rick

*Give me compassion, Lord, for all Your people. Open my eyes
and my heart to each problem. Help me understand every need.
Let Your compassion work through me. Amen.*

measure

God has allotted to each a measure of faith.
—Romans 12:3 NASB

Heavy rain threatened to cancel the evening outdoor performance of *Alice in Wonderland* my older sister, Georgia, was to perform in. It was midafternoon, and my younger sister, Ellen, who was about four at the time, overheard the conversation. She went to the closet, pulled her raincoat off the hanger, put on her rain boots, and asked my mother for the "big salt." Mom didn't understand at first, but finally realized that Ellen wanted the large container of Morton's Salt and handed it to her. Back in the seventies a popular Morton's Salt commercial featured a little girl who sprinkled salt, stopping the rain. Suited up in her rain gear, Ellen opened the back door, walked into the backyard, and started sprinkling salt, singing, "Rain, rain, go away, come again another day."

Little Ellen's measure of faith stopped the rain that day, and Georgia got to perform.

—Janet

Thanks, Lord, for a measure of faith. Amen.

opportunity

Be very careful, then, how you live—not as unwise but as wise, making the most of every opportunity.
—Ephesians 5:15–16 NIV

A notification appeared on my cell phone announcing my screen time was up 12 percent last week. Apparently, I spent an average of two hours and ten minutes each day texting, emailing, scrolling through social media, and surfing the Internet. I immediately justify my actions: communicating with family and friends, researching symptoms to convince my daughter she doesn't have a rare disease, shopping for a gift to welcome a new baby. Still, that notification stares at me like a little Holy Spirit inside my phone. I wonder if my prayer time was up 12 percent last week. Did I spend two hours reading my Bible? Do I make the most of every opportunity to fill myself with God's love and wisdom? The notification on my phone reminds me I can do better.

—Karen

Father, help me to spend less time online and more time with You. Amen.

confess

Therefore confess your sins to each other and pray for each other so that you may be healed. The prayer of a righteous person is powerful and effective.
—James 5:16 NIV

I grew up in a spiritual tradition that requires confession to clergy. When I was a kid, confession seemed ominous and scary. As I've matured in faith, I have a different understanding of this practice, particularly as James describes it. Sharing our failings with trusted brothers and sisters offers many benefits—surely what our Lord had in mind. We off-load feelings of shame and secrecy that can be toxic, often learning our friends have similar experiences. We can get practical advice—and accountability—to help us cope. We often get a sense of love and forgiveness, administered through our listener. We experience and affirm our equality as humble humans in need of grace.
—Isabella

Thank You, God, for urging James to give me this liberating and loving instruction. Grant me the courage to accept the invitation to confess. Amen.

rejoice

It is about your outlook towards life.
You can either regret or rejoice.
—Ralph Waldo Emerson

My beloved dad was a man of great exuberance. He had a booming baritone, a contagious laugh and a big generous smile. Daddy loved to sing in church, wax rhapsodic about the Scriptures, and oh, how he loved football. "Touchdooown!" he'd shout with glee. He loved to rejoice about all manner of things.

But there was much in his life not to rejoice about. He grew up during the Depression. When he was fourteen, his father died. He suffered other losses. Racism and bigotry were the order of the day, yet he prevailed, and he did not let anything stand in his way of becoming a doctor—a career he loved, and another reason to rejoice.

Daddy died at eighty-seven after a two-year illness. When Mom called to say he'd passed away, she added, "But, Jan! You should see the big smile on his face!"

—Janet

Lord, help me to rejoice and never regret. Amen.

miracles

Life is a series of a thousand tiny miracles. Notice them.
—Inspirational Christian quote

The tiny head peeping out of our birdhouse's rounded opening caught my eye. My husband and I delighted at this new life, full of possibility, until it jumped and attempted to fly. Instead, it careened downward. Not knowing what else to do, we placed it back into its home and hoped for the best. Days later, it looked fine.

Like that hatchling, I was helpless and vulnerable to all sorts of danger, until Jesus rescued me. One day I stood before my bathroom mirror. Something was different. I was staring into the face of a miracle, though I had no idea at the time. The life He'd laid out for me, full of baby birds and beaches, healing and hope, waited for me. A life filled with miracles. And I now have the eyes to see.

—Heidi

Lord, help me see the everyday miracles in my world. Amen.

forgive

A wise man will make haste to forgive.
—Samuel Johnson

H e meant it as a criticism, but I took it as a compliment. A Christian friend and I were having breakfast and discussing recent events in our lives, when my friend set down his fork, looked me in the eye, and said, "You're too quick to forgive." I think my mouth dropped open and I was at a loss for words for a few moments. Finally, I thanked him and said something like, "I hope that's always the case."

His comment still mystifies me, that a follower of Jesus—who in His most excruciating moment said, "Father, forgive them, for they do not know what they are doing" (Luke 23:34 NIV)—could say such a thing. I haven't always been true to his "criticism," as the deepest hurts tend to be the hardest to forgive. But I want to pray like Jesus, so I often pray, for myself and others around me: "Forgive."

—Bob

Father, forgive. Amen.

belong

Fear not, for I have redeemed you; I have called you by
your name; You are Mine.
—Isaiah 43:1 NKJV

When I look back on the firsts of my life—first day
of kindergarten, first day of college, first day on a
new job with a new company, first Sunday at a new
church—I remember the fear that I might not fit in. I looked
around at the people and wondered: Would I be accepted?
Did I belong, or would I forever be out of place?

In each of these instances, the thing that first set my mind at
ease was that one person—teacher, fellow student, friendly
coworker, church greeter—who welcomed me. Each one helped
me begin to see how I might belong.

Isaiah 43:1 tells me I belong to God. So I, in turn, want to be
among the first to make others feel they belong too.

—Jon

*Lord, thank You that I belong to You. Help me
pay forward Your gift of acceptance. Amen.*

hallowed

He said unto them, When ye pray, say, Our Father which art in heaven, Hallowed be thy name. Thy kingdom come.
—Luke 11:2 KJV

Growing up, my mother always encouraged me to learn poems and recite speeches in church. My Sunday-school teacher also helped me memorize various Scriptures. I was so incredibly proud of myself when I memorized the Lord's Prayer, one of the most treasured passages in the Bible. Years later, the Lord's Prayer still flowed effortlessly from my tongue, but as my Bible teacher discussed each line of the prayer, I realized that I didn't really understand some of the prayer's deeper meanings. The phrase "Hallowed be your name, your kingdom come" touched my heart. That night I learned that hallowed means to be honored and set apart as holy, respected, and glorified. God's name is holy and worthy of all the honor, glory, and praise I can give.

—Rosalind

Father, help me to hallow Your name every day. Amen.

street

As we have therefore opportunity, let us do good unto all men, especially unto them who are of the household of faith.
—Galatians 6:10 KJV

One morning while walking in my neighborhood, I saw two women talking. I introduced myself and joined their conversation. One lady asked about a church, so I gave her the name of the church I attended and let her know I would be out of town the following Sunday. After we exchanged numbers, she said, "Please, let's connect when you return." We did, and just like that, we became early-morning walking buddies. Soon after, she and her family joined our church. Estelle and I call each other "street friend." We knew our meeting was a divine appointment because she usually walks at 6:00 a.m. and I walk at 11:00 a.m. She was late that day, but it turned out she was right on time. Blessed connections can happen in the street.

—Penne

Thank You, God, for giving us new friends in unlikely places. Amen.

encourage

The light shines in the darkness, and
the darkness has not overcome it.
—John 1:5 NIV

When our kids were young, my husband, Kevin, and I attended a workshop on effective communication with teens. Over twenty years later, I can remember only one phrase from those eight hours of teaching: "When you are tempted to feel like a failure, tell yourself, 'I make more miracles than messes.'" Saying those words encouraged me to focus on the bright stars of family jokes and healthy conversations rather than the dark nights of misunderstandings. My daughter now is raising three teens of her own. I love to encourage her and tell her, "Remember, you make more miracles than messes." The stars reflecting from her eyes are my hug and kiss from God.

—Jeanette

*Lord, I used to think encouragement was a trivial gift,
until I needed a huge dose. Help me freely share it
with those in dark times. Amen.*

wheel

Jesus, take the wheel.
—Popular saying/prayer

I t's one of my favorite sayings, popularized in the 2005 hit song performed by Carrie Underwood. The lyrics tell of a young woman, her life filled with terrible troubles, driving along a snowy road on Christmas Eve with her baby sleeping in the back seat. Going way too fast, she hits a patch of black ice and sees both their lives flash before her eyes. "Jesus, take the wheel," she cries. "Save me from this road I'm on."

In the years since the song was released, the phrase has become widely used. Sometimes it's a sincere request for divine intervention. Other times, it's a lighthearted plea for help. For me, it's always a prayer. I pray the words not only when the eighteen-wheelers are barreling past me on the highway, but also any time I'm tense or worried or afraid. I'm grateful I don't have to steer the icy patches alone.

—Jennie

Jesus, take the wheel. Amen.

eulogy

*The minister related many a touching incident
in the lives of the departed.*
—Mark Twain, *The Adventures of Tom Sawyer*

Who among us has not fantasized about attending our own funeral? The idea came to me at an early age when I read *Tom Sawyer* for the first time. Presumed drowned, Tom and two friends sneak into church and listen to the wonderful things being said about them during their funeral. They delight in seeing their loved ones prostrate with grief. The scene has stuck with me for more than fifty years. It's funny, but also life-altering.

As a senior citizen, I know I have more years behind me than ahead of me. From time to time, I think about my own funeral. And I try to live so that whoever delivers my eulogy will genuinely have kind things to say.

—Jennie

*Father, help me live in such a way that good words spoken
at my funeral will be true. Amen.*

provision

Look at the birds of the air; they do not sow or reap or store away in barns, and yet your heavenly Father feeds them. Are you not much more valuable than they?
—Matthew 6:26 NIV

D
on't throw that away!" my mother yelled. I paused and double-checked the expiration date on the loaf of bread I was holding. It was expired, but to Mom it was perfect. She reminded me that the secret to her amazing bread pudding is old, slightly stale bread, just like the bread we feed birds. It's still nourishing, and they're happy for the provision. I marveled that when resources seem to expire, God in His infinite wisdom always knows how to mix together just what's needed, and just in time. He always provides.

—Ty'Ann

Thank You, Lord, for Your provision when it seems I've exhausted my resources. Everything I need is in You, so I trust in You, my great Shepherd. Amen.

move

Life is like riding a bicycle. To keep your balance,
you must keep moving.
—Albert Einstein

My parents had one rule when it came to learning to ride a bike: no training wheels. So they helped me onto the bike, adjusted my feet on the pedals, and held the back of the seat to steady me as I began to pedal. They guided the bike as I rode, wobbling and weaving, and then they would let go.

After falling and getting up again and again, I was thrilled to discover I was riding on my own!

Eventually I understood my parents' mindset. Life doesn't come with training wheels, but it does come with a loving God Who gets me in position, steadies me, guides me, dusts me off when I fall, and then encourages me to try again and keep moving, helping me to fly.

—Janet

Dear God, thank You for helping and balancing me, keeping me on the move. Amen.

whisper

And after the earthquake a fire; but the Lᴏʀᴅ was
not in the fire: and after the fire a still small voice.
—1 Kings 19:12 KJV

I have a lot of favorite things, but one that stands at the very top is my tiny granddaughter calling me Pop Pop. Granted, she's not even a year old and just learning to talk, so consonants don't always come out like they're supposed to, but I sure hear it clear enough.

My very, very favorite is when she whispers (she loves to whisper). It's so precious. Just between us. Intimate and perfect.

I think that's why God often speaks to His children in that still, small voice. Just between us. Intimate. Perfect. Like I do with my granddaughter, when He whispers, I have to still myself. I have to listen. Lean in.

Right where I should have been all along.

—Buck

Thank You, God, that Your still, small voice thunders over this world's pathetic din. Amen.

why

He who has a why to live for can bear almost any how.
—Friedrich Nietzsche

When my dad passed away, I wanted to know why. Why did God think I was ready to be without an earthly father? Why wouldn't my dad get to meet my future kids? Why did God think this was okay? I wrestled with God a lot that year, feeling anger and apathy at turns. It wasn't until, years later, that I had a child who hated the car seat, screaming every time I tried to snap him in. "I'm so sorry I can't take you out of this. I'll sit right beside you until we get there, though." In that moment, it clicked. I may never know the why, but now I know that, while God may not take me out of a situation, He sits in it with me.

—Ashley

Lord, help me remember that You are sovereign,
even when I'm hurting. Amen.

butter

Life is too short for fake butter.
—Julia Child

When I was a child, my family spread oleomargarine—commonly called "oleo"—on biscuits and cornbread and a whole lot of other food. Margarine, invented in the 1860s to be cheaper and less perishable than butter, was originally made with beef fat. Later, it was manufactured with hydrogenated vegetable oil and a long list of other ingredients. Margarine was sold softened and packaged in plastic tubs and also in solid sticks. Decades passed before nutritionists concluded that butter, made from nothing but real cream, was healthier than margarine. "If you can't pronounce the ingredients on the margarine label, you probably shouldn't eat it," they said.

There's a lot to be said for choosing real and simple over fake and complicated. Especially when it comes to faith. I choose a faith with a simple list of rules: Love God. Love your neighbor. Love yourself.

—Jennie

Help me, Father, to be genuine in all that I say and do. Amen.

inheritance

We are all gifted. That is our inheritance.
—Ethel Waters

My parents died penniless. I did inherit some lovely jewelry, art, books, and furniture. I'm grateful, but cash would have been nice. Or would it? We've all seen stories about trust-fund kids who never fulfill their potential or, worse, live a dissipated life, never maturing. The money isn't the problem. The complacent comfort the money provides seems to prevent personal growth.

The Bible talks a lot about spiritual inheritance and untold gifts of incomparable power, love, wisdom, and grace independent of anything material. These treasures serve me here and in eternity, but with eternal value at great odds with this world. Likewise, the truly valuable things I inherited from my parents were talents and characteristics that have served me more than any stock portfolio. I would have liked both, but God's truth reminds me what matters and why.

—Isabella

God, let me fully appreciate the intangible inheritance I have from my earthly parents and from You, my Heavenly Father. Amen.

glitter

Sprinkle a little glitter wherever you go.
—Pinterest poster

Whenever I visited my grandmother in her nursing home, I liked to take a small gift. Sometimes food. Sometimes a bouquet of wildflowers. Sometimes an item that struck my fancy at the dollar store. One day a display of inexpensive nail polishes caught my eye. I pondered the color choices. Pale pink? Too boring. Dark purple? Too ghoulish. Then I saw it. Gold glitter. Perfect.

Grandmother was sitting at the jigsaw puzzle table when I arrived that afternoon. "Look what I brought," I said. Talking was hard for her, but her eyes lit up as she laid her hands flat on the table, fingers spread. In no time at all, her hands sparkled. Soon, another patient rolled her wheelchair over to ask if it was her turn. Half an hour later, every woman in the commons area—including me—was wearing gold glitter nail polish.

And gigantic smiles.

—Jennie

Heavenly Father, help me to spread joy wherever I can. Amen.

optimism

Why, my soul, are you downcast? Why so disturbed
within me? Put your hope in God, for I will yet praise
him, my Savior and my God.
—Psalm 43:5 NIV

wouldn't call myself a pessimist, but I *can* often see one
hundred reasons why a thing can't be done. I've had to train
my mind to focus on why something *is* possible. As a result,
I'm accomplishing things in my middle age that I wouldn't have
dreamed of when I was younger.

When I experienced crippling self-doubt years ago, a friend
once quoted Henry Ford saying, "Whether you think you can or
you think you can't, you're right." I can be my own worst critic
or my own best cheerleader. When I put my hope in God, I can
step out in faith, full of optimism even in the challenging times.

—Jon

Lord, when I am paralyzed by uncertainty,
help me put my hope in You. Amen.

humility

Therefore, whoever takes the lowly position of this child
is the greatest in the kingdom of heaven.
—Matthew 18:4 NIV

I stood patiently outside the arena. It was crowded and drizzling, but neither would deter me from the opportunity to meet Oprah Winfrey. I was at the front of the gated area, and suddenly there she was, walking toward me. It was really happening—I was on the verge of being up close with Oprah! I'm from New York City so I'm used to seeing celebrities, but Oprah was a big deal. My hands were shaking, and I was nearly speechless. I managed to get a selfie with her. Birthday made! But then it hit me. I'd been humbled in the presence of human greatness, but my humility in this situation was no match for the awe and reverence I have for Jesus. After all, He's King.

—Ty'Ann

What an honor to humble myself before You, Jesus, the Savior of the world. May nothing deter me from Your awe-filled presence. Amen.

work

Work is a blessing. God has so arranged the world that work is necessary, and He gives us hands and strength to do it.
—Elisabeth Elliot

When the demands of my job feel stressful, I sometimes find myself looking forward to my next day off when I can indulge in some leisure time and shrug off the challenges of work. It's easy to think of my job, and even my personal chores, negatively, as being the punishment for Adam and Eve's wrongdoing that still affects me today! While God did say work would be harder after the fall, work was part of His original plan for us (Gen. 2:15), not the result of our broken relationship. Though God also recommends regular opportunities to rest and provided the Sabbath, I can choose to look at my work—at home or in the world—as a joyful opportunity to fulfill the purpose He's given me.

—Kirsten

Thank You, God, for giving me the privilege of work. Amen.

before

And the name of the city from that day shall be,
the LORD is there.
—Ezekiel 48:35 KJV

A s I was contemplating moving to a new city, I prayed for confirmation—was I making the right move? God spoke very clearly to me through Ezekiel 48:35. The words, "The LORD is there," assured me that God had gone before me and all would be well.

Years after I had settled in that new city, a fellow nurse was moving away. At her farewell party she shared that she was concerned about moving to an unfamiliar place, just as I'd been. So I shared my story of how God had gone before me and prepared the way, and had taken care of everything. He even made sure I'd have friends who would become like family. Now, I know with assurance that wherever I go, God goes before me.

—Penne

Dear Lord, thank You for going before me and preparing the way. Amen.

hear

Your voice is my favorite sound.
—lovequotes.com

'm a big fan of text messaging. It's quick, easy, and especially handy when making a phone call is inconvenient. Though I was nearly fifty years old the first time I sent a text, I saw its value right off the bat.

But as time passed and my children grew up and moved out on their own, texts from them almost completely replaced phone calls. Ditto for my siblings and many of my friends. So I vowed to make at least one quick no-real-reason phone call every day. I'm still at it. Sometimes I get an answer. (Yay!) Sometimes I get voice mail. When that happens, my message is always the same. "Hey," I say. "I just called to hear your sweet voice."

The reply when they call me back? "I want to hear your sweet voice too."

—Jennie

Thank You, God, for telephones—and for the sweet voices of those I love. Amen.

rise

You may shoot me with your words, you may cut me
with your eyes, you may kill me with your hatefulness,
but still, like air, I'll rise!
—Maya Angelou

The woman's email made it clear she disliked me. The part that hurt most was her attack on my faith. My blood pressure skyrocketed. Had I unknowingly done something to anger this woman? *What should I do next?* After rereading the message, I leaned back in my chair, closed my eyes and asked for guidance.

The answer to my prayer didn't come that minute or the next. But as I went about my day, Jesus's peace slowly replaced the hurt, and by evening, my joy was returning. Like many trials we encounter, I had to decide where I stood. Would I focus on negativity or rise above it? Early the next morning, I deleted the email. I'd made my choice. Like the sun, I'd rise.

—Heidi

*God, on tough days give me the strength—and
the positivity—to rise. Amen.*

speak

Speak, LORD, for your servant is listening.
—1 Samuel 3:9 NIV

One of my most treasured possessions is a recording. My parents and I lived in St. Louis while my brother and his wife were attending school in New York City. Every week or two, rather than writing letters, we would record a cassette tape and mail it back and forth. None of us knew that my mother would be in heaven months later, but one of those recordings of her speaking and playing the church organ survives. To hear her speak, not only across space but also through time—and eternity—is a blessing.

Something similar happens as I open my Bible to read each day. I usually pray the single word "Speak," sometimes audibly, sometimes silently, to invite God to transcend time and space and speak from eternity into my little life. And He does, often, movingly, as I read not for mere information but for true communion.

—Bob

Speak, Lord, for Your servant is listening. Amen.

family

My mother used to tell me that when push comes to shove, you always know who to turn to. That being a family isn't a social construct but an instinct.

—Jodi Picoult

I have no idea where I would be without my family. Whenever we're together we have a great time. When we have parties, we don't just invite a *few* people. We invite *everyone*. A small event turns large quickly. I'm lucky to be part of a family that genuinely wants to be together, not just because we share blood.

But friends can become family too. So I have a few families. My crazy relatives who gather not because they have to but because they want to. And the friends who chose to let me in and who I let in, in return. Even when you think you don't need family, they're there anyway.

—Sabrina

Thank You, God, for giving me more than one family.
I would be lost without them. Amen.

stop

Don't hurry. Don't worry. You're only here for a short visit. So
don't forget to stop and smell the roses.
—Walter Hagen

'm a driven, type-A person. Few things make me happier
than crossing off items on my to-do list. My stress level builds
anytime I feel myself falling behind. And yet the times I feel
closest to God are not when I'm most productive, but when
I'm doing absolutely nothing. When I make myself stop, let my
mind go blank, and listen to a world that goes otherwise unno-
ticed. "Be still and know that I am God," the psalmist wrote. In
other words, stop. One day I hope it will come naturally to me,
but until then, I'm making time to stop doing part of each day's
to-do list.

—Evan

*Dear God, teach me to learn to stop and listen
for Your voice. Amen.*

emotion

There can be no transforming of darkness into light and of apathy into movement without emotion.
—Carl Jung

E motions are a funny thing, aren't they? Someone is considered emotional if they cry too much, but not if they get angry. In science fiction, the alien race is often considered unemotional, even though they're portrayed as proud, easily irritated, and angry. But anger, pride, and irritation are emotions—just like joy, grief, and sympathy. Am I more comfortable feeling afraid or angry? (Angry.) Angry or sad? (Angry.) Sad or happy? (Happy.) What feelings do I try to hide most from others? Every emotion I have is telling me something. I probably ought to listen to all of them.

—Meg

Lord, You created every emotion, and You had Your reasons for them all. Let me see Your reflection in everything I'm feeling.
Amen.

understanding

O Divine Master, grant that I may not so much seek to be
consoled as to console, to be understood, as to understand.
—St. Francis

During my first year of college, I dated a young man I'll
call Peter. Peter's definition of understanding contrasted
mine by a mile. When I stated a different opinion from
his, Peter always said, "You don't understand." He reminded
me of a child, hands on hips, who insists that using sand is the
only way to build a castle. I realized Peter wanted an echo, not
a relationship. We broke up. The following year I married a
man who appreciated my unique point of view. That was over
forty years ago. Now, when I accuse my husband of not understanding me, God brings Peter to mind. It's His gentle reminder
that castles are created from a variety of materials. And all are
exquisite in their own way.

—Jeanette

*Lord, help me understand others' viewpoints and
applaud the differences. Amen.*

wisdom

A good head and a good heart are always
a formidable combination.
—Nelson Mandela

Until I was older, I didn't realize just how wise my mother (Ma) and grandmother (Mama) were in preparing me for a successful and meaningful life. Their approaches were different, but certainly complementary and compatible. Saturdays were the key. Ma arranged for academic enrichment and advanced instruction on many Saturday mornings. She didn't know how to drive but secured transportation so I could participate. Ma diligently cultivated the potential she saw in me. Mama conducted Bible study at her house almost every Saturday evening. Whichever grandchildren were visiting or spending the night at her home participated. Period. On summer evenings, at dusk, during prime outdoor playtime, we grandkids came inside. Mama knew we needed the spiritual enrichment that she could readily provide.

I'm who I am today because of the wisdom Ma and Mama exercised, and instilled in me.

—Steve

Thank You, Lord, for people who shower us with love and wisdom.

covenant

My covenant of peace shall not be removed.
—Isaiah 54:10 ESV

Covenant is serious business with God. Not just a promise that might be kept, one offered easily until distraction or convenience or something more important interferes. I've found myself there more than once. With God I can count on nothing getting in the way. Because when God covenants, He backs it up with Himself. His own unchanging faithfulness. This is the story of Jesus—God's Son coming to the world for every single person who opens their heart to Him. Even when saving others meant losing His own life. He even kept covenant beyond the cross—rising to give me His unending life! God and I have a covenant—my trust, His peace.

—Carol

A covenant relationship with You, God of Your word, is my greatest peace. Amen.

future

Never be afraid to trust an unknown future to a known God.
—Corrie ten Boom

I was forty-three years old when I met the love of my life. I had never married and was pretty sure I'd never meet "Mr. Right." But Bob was just right for me; I called him my present from God. Shortly after our tenth anniversary, Bob had a routine surgery. Within weeks, he was dead. I felt like my life had ended too.

But I was wrong. It's been nearly twelve years since Bob died. Do I miss him? Of course. But God has given me amazing blessings over the last dozen years. I've moved to the beach, a lifelong dream. I have a new "family" in Haiti: sixty-three orphans who are learning to trust their futures to their loving heavenly Father.

God still has plans and a good future for me—and for you.
—Michelle

Thank You, Lord, that You hold my future in Your loving, compassionate hands. Amen.

star

Only in the darkness can you see the stars.
—Martin Luther King Jr.

Years ago, I bought one of my favorite souvenirs while I was visiting Paris with my sister, Jenny. In the corner of a quaint little shop, I found a simple papier-mâché star with a black, jeweled center. It was the perfect reminder of Paris's beauty.

There is nothing more beautiful than a star. Stars are symbols of hope. Their light travels to earth from trillions of miles away, lighting the darkest of nights. Millions of new stars are born every day, reminding me that I am not alone. Each star is placed there by a loving Creator. A singular star marked the birth of His only Son, sent to save the world, revealing the hope that all of creation longed for. His name? Jesus. The Bright and Morning Star.

—Susanna

Jesus, as I see the stars each night, let them remind me that I am not alone and that I have hope in You. Amen.

let

Let go and let God.
—Anonymous

I n the bright light of retrospect, I realized I have cleaved to a few things in life long after God was done with them and was inviting me to release them. People, ideas, projects, beliefs, jobs, coping mechanisms, and the occasional outdated article of clothing. At the time, I could have made the case for why I held on so tightly that it hurt me and others. Sometimes, my reasons seemed holy to me and I'd pray about it. Then I'd promptly interject my own misguided idea of Bible teaching to justify my tight grip rather than listening to what God had to say. Other times, my ego didn't want to admit defeat, or I couldn't let go of worn-out phrases like "No pain, no gain." I've finally figured out a better way. Ask God, then listen with my heart. Listen for His loving answer, and then let go.

—Isabella

Dear Jesus, help me release my grip on whoever, whatever, in love. Amen.

wallow

I would not have traded the delights of
my suffering for anything in the world.
—Gabriel Garcia Marquez

So many times, I have pushed through disappointment, frustration, and loss. But when my dad died, I simply couldn't. For weeks, I would break down in fits of tears in random locations: in the shower, on bike rides, getting the mail. Finally, I realized that despite my tears, I was still trying to push through. *Okay, let's do this,* I thought. I gave into my suffering, my heartbreak, and my sorrow, allowing myself to admit that I couldn't get past my pain until I really sat in it awhile. Eventually, I could see a glimmer of light, then finally an open window. Today, I don't need to wallow any longer, but I know it was the act of sitting still that allowed me to get up and move forward again.

—Ashley

Lord, help me take the time I need to process whatever situation comes into my life. Amen.

unburden

Come to me, all you who are weary and burdened,
and I will give you rest.
—Matthew 11:28 NIV

I had been battling cancer for a few years and eventually had to start doing follow-up scans. I would always get worried and anxious before an appointment, especially on the way there. Then one day, on one of those trips to the cancer center, I unburdened myself to God. I did not care what the taxi driver thought. I just cried out to God, from the depth of my heart, and with raw honesty, shared all my fears and worries. I told God everything I was feeling. I spilled it all! The cancer did not go away at that moment or even that year, but in unburdening myself I found rest.

—Didi

Lord, I unburden myself to You. Jesus, You are my best friend, and I can be completely honest with You. Amen.

hope

Now may the God of hope fill you with all joy
and peace in believing, that you may abound
in hope by the power of the Holy Spirit.
—Romans 15:13 NKJV

When I was four years old, I loved the Pillsbury commercial that featured the Poppin' Fresh Doughboy miraculously popping out of a roll of biscuits when you cracked open the container. One day my mother left me in the kitchen with a grocery bag. A few minutes later, she found me surrounded by open biscuit containers. I said hopefully, "I'm looking for the doughboy!"

My hope waned when I was in my thirties. During that time, my parents came for a visit, and my dad bought a Pillsbury Doughboy doll in the airport gift shop. He didn't offer an explanation when he gave it to me, but I was grateful for the reminder.

A few weeks later, I placed my hope in Jesus, the One Who can always be found.

—Janet

Thanks, Lord, for abounding hope in You. Amen.

door

God enters by a private door into every individual.
—Ralph Waldo Emerson

Doors show up quite a bit in Scripture. Jesus refers to Himself as a door. In fact, in John 10:9, Jesus says He is the door to salvation and pasture, which I interpret as provision of all kinds. I find it helps me understand spiritual concepts better when I relate them to everyday life. Doors enable me to move from place to place, from space to space. Doors let me gain access to what I want or need. Doors also keep out unwanted visitors. Doors protect against the elements or intruders. Doors can be closed to block out light or noise. My old house had too many entry doors, which confused visitors all the time.

Are you getting the picture? Jesus is the door—the only door—to everything we want and need. Likewise, He's the protection against the unwanted. He is *the* door.

—Isabella

Jesus, thank You for being the door to me and all humanity.
Amen.

gracious

Therefore, the LORD longs to be gracious to you, and
therefore, He waits on high to have mercy on you; for the
LORD is a God of justice; how blessed are all who long for Him.
—Isaiah 30:18 MEV

I was thrilled when I looked up "Jeanette" in a baby name
book and discovered it means "God is gracious." *Wow, I
thought, every time someone says my name they're declaring how kind, generous, and merciful the Lord is.* But I wasn't
satisfied. Those three words didn't hold enough meaning
to describe God's endless affection for His children. When I
researched the word in its original Hebrew, *hesed*, I read "disposed to show favors." Ahhh...that's better. The Lord gives me
all I need and much of what I want not because He's obligated.
He encourages and helps and forgives because that's His
nature. He simply can't help Himself.

—Jeanette

*What a marvelous God You are, to enjoy lavishing
favors on me. I appreciate You! Amen.*

sweeten

Sweet are the uses of adversity.
—William Shakespeare

I recently adopted a new nutritional regimen and eliminated sugar (other than that found naturally in unprocessed foods) entirely from my diet. In the process I discovered that several strawberries or blueberries (rather than heaping teaspoons of sugar) more than adequately sweetened a bowl of oatmeal or a fresh salad.

I think my spiritual life works in a similar way. I'd like it if every activity or incident in my day were sweet and easy, but even if it were possible, it wouldn't be best. I know that flat tires, computer glitches, unscheduled interruptions, and other dangers and difficulties are bound to come. But I pray for God to sweeten my troubles and trials with His presence and power, and He often does. Sometimes He even transforms them into unexpected blessings.

—Bob

*God, please sweeten my troubles and trials with
Your presence and power today. Amen.*

vine

I am the vine; you are the branches...apart
from me you can do nothing.
—John 15:5 NIV

I was excited to move to our new home across town, but sad to leave behind my favorite plant, a beautiful and somewhat rare variety of clematis. After unsuccessfully scouring the local nurseries to purchase another one, I resorted to trimming off a few branches in hopes of transplanting them to my new yard. Despite my best efforts to root and plant them, the branches withered and died. While a more skilled gardener might have succeeded, this frustrating experience reminded me of how I need to remain connected to Jesus, the Vine who sustains and supports me, apart from whom I can do nothing. Best of all, the Vine holds on to its branches—not the other way around—making me both secure and fruitful.

—Kirsten

Jesus, thank You for being the Vine that secures and sustains me and brings forth fruit in my life. Amen.

harvest

While the earth remaineth, seedtime and harvest,
and cold and heat, and summer and winter,
and day and night shall not cease.
—Genesis 8:22 KJV

I grew up in a small town where my dad was one of many farmers. He would rise early each morning, enjoy a hearty breakfast, and off to the field he went. In the spring, he plowed the field and planted cottonseeds. The cotton grew and so did the weeds. My dad hired field hands to chop the cotton to rid it of weeds. By summer it was time to harvest the crop, and the same field hands came back to pick the cotton.

God works that same process of planting and sowing in my life as I read His Word, which goes down into the soil of my heart, where it reaps a harvest of love and other good things to share.

—Rosalind

Father, thank You for seedtime and harvest, and
for Your abundant grace that never ends. Amen.

resilience

Life has two rules: number 1, never quit! Number 2,
always remember rule number 1.
—Duke Ellington

After six years traveling the world as a professional soccer player, the last three as a local celebrity, I was a twenty-seven-year-old staffer in a new and intensely demanding competitive industry. Now, I was simply a *former* professional athlete—and it took some time for me to adjust to that qualifier. I felt awkward. My work peers were recent college grads, and my chronological peers were already two to three levels ahead in the organization. *And,* I was the only one of my college buddies who wasn't yet married. Work was challenging, but I stuck it out, relying on the Lord and on the resilience I'd developed as an athlete earlier in life. Soon enough I made it through those thorny times, moved on professionally, and through a former client, met the lady I'd marry.

—Steve

Thank You, Lord, for a resilience that comes from you. Amen.

confirmation

Thou wilt shew me the path of life: in thy presence is fulness
of joy; at thy right hand there are pleasures for evermore.
—Psalm 16:11 KJV

As I wrestled with a decision to go back into the workplace as a nurse during the COVID-19 pandemic, my thoughts overwhelmed me. Should I go back into the emergency department, in harm's way? I prayed with a friend about my dilemma and she read Psalm 16 to me. The final verse, verse 11, gave me confidence that God would show me the path I was to take. Later that day on a brief teleconference, the pastor who delivered the message talked about Psalm 16:11! I felt as if God had whispered confirmation that He would show me the right path in an unsure season. Sure enough, joy and blessings followed.

—Penne

*Dear Lord, thank You for confirming Your Word
and showing me the path to take. Amen.*

hide

Hide me in the shadow of your wings.
—Psalm 17:8 NIV

'd heard and seen a hummingbird flying around our door, but I was nonetheless surprised to discover a tiny nest in the branches of the tree that overhangs our front sidewalk. The nest, about the diameter of a quarter or half-dollar coin and sheltered by the leaves of the tree, hides two baby humming-birds. The hummingbird mom jets back and forth from the nest, bringing food and protecting the babies under her wings.

It's a tiny reminder of the psalmist's prayer ("Hide me in the shadow of your wings") and the songwriter's plea: ("Hide me, O my Savior, hide, Till the storm of life is past" (Charles Wesley). It's my prayer and plea, too, to be sheltered by God as a mother bird shelters her brood.

—Bob

Lord, hide me in the shadow of Your wings today and every day. Amen.

nervous

She is clothed with strength and dignity, and she laughs
without fear of the future.
—Proverbs 31:25 NLT

've always found a way to make myself nervous before there's
ever a reason to be. My mind gets revved up and zooms to
all the "what-ifs" that *could* happen weeks, months, or even
years into the future. Frequently, I have to catch myself and
stop my mind from running wild. I remind myself that there's no
reason to be nervous about things that may not ever happen.
It's a waste of my energy worrying about a situation that isn't in
my control currently and may never be fully. My time is better
spent focusing on the present, without fear of the future.

—Jaylin

*Lord, please help me remember that there's no need to be
nervous when You're in control of my future. Amen.*

exhale

The healthiest response to life is joy.
—Deepak Chopra

do it without even knowing. Exhale, followed by inhale and then exhale again. How many times a minute do I exhale? Two? Ten? When I release my breath and really exhale, I feel a sense of calm and peace, of resetting my mind and body to be poised for whatever comes next.

This morning I had a frustrating email exchange with a colleague. I can feel the stress in my shoulders and neck as I reread the conversation.

Exhale, I remind myself—breathe deep, then let it out. Letting go of the air also lets go of the negative, the frustration.

—Carolyn

God, as I exhale, help me to remember to turn my frustration and worries over to You so that I feel Your love and peace no matter the situation. Amen.

grace

But he said to me, "My grace is sufficient for you, for my power is made perfect in weakness."
—2 Corinthians 12:9 NIV

Many years ago, when I was a nursing student, I came to a point of sheer exhaustion before a biochemistry test. I hadn't studied at all and it was literally just before midnight. My friend and I had planned an all-night study vigil. Just before she arrived at my dorm room, I called my mother and shared my dilemma. She said simply, "Go to bed. I'll pray for you." Those were the sweetest words she could have said to my groggy body. She was right. I needed rest. Suddenly I felt at peace, as if God Himself had spoken through my mother.

When my friend knocked on my door, I told her what my mom had said. Then I went to sleep. By God's grace I passed the test.

—Penne

Dear God, thank You for grace and a praying mother. Amen.

delight

Then I was constantly at his side. I was filled with delight day
after day, rejoicing always in his presence.
—Proverbs 8:30 NIV

I wonder if I enjoy caffeine a bit too much. Ten minutes into
my stationary bike ride this morning, I craved a refill of rasp-
berry tea. Whenever I bike, my husband, Kevin, always pops
in to refill my mug from the pot he's brewed. But this morning,
he'd already kissed me goodbye on his way to Bible study. I
thought he'd left. When I saw him walk through the bedroom
door, I clapped like a four-year-old at the circus. Kev held only
his Bible—no teapot. Embarrassment heated my cheeks. "I'm
sorry, honey. I should be more delighted to see you than I am
to get a refill." Yes, just as delighted as I long to feel in God's
presence, whether He gives me anything or not.

—Jeanette

*Dear Lord, You are my highest delight. I love You more than
caffeine, kittens, or chocolate. Amen.*

if

The "what ifs" and "should haves" will eat your brain.
—John O'Callaghan

If. Such a tiny word, but at times, the bane of my existence. At different times in my life it's been quite the stumbling block. *If* I get that job, or house, I'll be happy. *If* I could only solve that problem, I'd relax. *If* only my childhood had been better, I'd be better. So many conditions for the outcome I think I want. As I've gotten older, many of my ifs have been fulfilled, with a whole new crop emerging. Other ifs never happened, threatening to leave a wound that wouldn't heal. At some point, my discomfort with this undeniable reality led me to find a better way. *If* I simply trust Jesus's utter sufficiency, the other ifs will become less weighty. I can truly enjoy my reality no matter what, finally free of the endless pursuit of fruitless *ifs*.

—Isabella

Jesus, provide for me the deepest sense that
You alone will handle all my ifs. Amen.

truth

Kids do say the darndest things
—Art Linkletter

O ur wonderful, weekend getaway with our dear family
friends was almost over. Their youngest child cleared
his throat and cautiously, yet confidently said (in his
high-pitched grade-school voice), "Mr. Steve, I don't mean any
harm." He then took a brief, thoughtful pause. "But if you and your
wife don't have any children yet, then why is your hair gray?"
Between smiles, laughter, and a few playful, wrestling hugs,
I gently explained premature graying. I told him that it ran in
my family and acknowledged that yep, even though I was in
my mid-thirties, I had a lot of gray hair. Finally, I reassured him
lovingly and graciously that it's good to speak the truth, and
that no harm (offense) had been taken.

—Steve

*Lord, let us be as open to hearing the truth about ourselves from
children as they are willing to share it with us. Amen.*

snow

Cleanse me with hyssop, and I will be clean;
wash me, and I will be whiter than snow.
—Psalm 51:7 NIV

I love a clean layer of brilliant white snow covering the ground. It creates a winter wonderland. Growing up in Illinois, I loved playing in the snow, building forts, and making snow angels in the soft, white powder. What I didn't love was encountering the dirty, melted snow lining the roads. There was nothing worse than stepping off a curb and feeling your boot fill with brown, watery slush. That is snow gone wrong.

Sometimes my heart feels like a brown slush pile of snow gone wrong. There is nothing worse than the remnants of sin, anxiety, and selfishness coloring the edges of my life. I need to be cleaned up. I need Jesus's mercy and grace to wash me clean as only He can. His forgiveness purifies my soul whiter than snow.

—Susanna

Jesus, please forgive my sins and wash me whiter than snow. Amen.

roads

Every valley shall be filled in, every mountain and hill made low. The crooked roads shall become straight, the rough ways smooth.
—Luke 3:5 NIV

My daughter gripped the steering wheel during her first attempt to drive our Ozark roads that wind up and down and around sharp curves. We approached a hill. "Hit the gas now so you can maintain speed on the incline," I advised. I taught her to use the accelerator rather than the brake to slow for a curve and then speed up to maneuver through it. These roads that posed danger for an inexperienced driver would soon lead my daughter away from home to unfamiliar roads with many twists, presenting new and different dangers. My time in the passenger seat was limited. What had I taught her about handling life's ups and downs, about facing unexpected curves? I prayed I had prepared her to travel the crooked roads safely.

—Karen

Father, straighten the roads our children travel and lead them always to You. Amen.

blessings

Every good gift and every perfect gift is from above, and cometh down from the Father of lights, with whom is no variableness, neither shadow of turning.

—James 1:17 KJV

My husband and I are currently looking to purchase a home. We've seen hundreds of homes, and each time we put in an offer we're outbid. Recently we thought we'd found our home. *The One!* But the night before our appointment another offer was accepted. At first, we were heartbroken, but God quickly blessed us with deep peace.

God's blessings come in many forms. Mostly through answered prayers, but also in prayers that are not answered, or not answered according to our timetable. I've come to learn that blessings that touch my heart the deepest are those that, at first glance, may not look like a blessing at all.

—Didi

Thank You, Jesus, that although I might not know "the why," I do know You, and You bless me in ways I don't always understand. Amen.

dare

Those who dare to fail miserably can achieve greatly.
—John F. Kennedy

I can't do it!" James yelled. At four, James, who can swim, often had to be talked into things, including going to Disney World, trying cake, and, apparently, jumping into a lake while wearing a life jacket. We've learned that sometimes we need to push him to try, or else he misses out. "I can't!" he continued. "I'm too scared!" I swam closer to him. "Then be scared!" I said, "and do it anyway!" His brow furrowed as he considered my words. And then he jumped...as much as you can jump from a float that's directly on the water. Then he did it again, and again, and *again*. Later, when he was snuggled in a warm towel, I asked him what his highlight of the day was. "Jumping in, Mama," he said. Sometimes, I need to dare to get my best reward.

—Ashley

Lord, give me the confidence to trust in You always. Amen.

fresh

Every moment is a fresh beginning.
—T.S. Eliot

Fresh starts are important to me. One of my favorites is the start of a new day. Some days are long, heavy, and drag on to the point that I'm exhausted by evening and stressed out about what tomorrow might bring. Instead of dwelling on that, I encourage myself to believe that tomorrow can be a fresh start. An apology can bring a fresh start in a relationship. Moving can initiate a fresh start in achieving a dream. Fresh starts allow me to see problems or stressors with a new perspective. A way to reset my mind one hundred percent to allow me the same strength I had at the start of my journey.

—Jaylin

Lord, allow me to see all the fresh starts You have available for me throughout my journey. Amen.

silence

Silence is holy. It draws people together because only those who are comfortable with each other can sit without speaking. This is the great paradox.
—Nicholas Sparks

My wife, Carol, and I are lounging around the house on a Sunday afternoon. I lie on the bed, reading. She picks up a book. I check a message on my phone, then stare out the window, watching the clouds. For an hour we are silent. No phone conversations, no talking. Comfortable silence. I can be with those I love and be silent. It's like when I wake up every morning and close my eyes, checking in with God. Silly things pop into my head. God understands. We share a comfortable, reassuring silence because He knows I trust and believe in Him.

—Rick

Help me shut up, Lord, and listen to You. You know my deepest needs and wants better than I do. When all the noise in my head quiets down, there's nothing but You. Blessed silence. Amen.

altar

And Moses built an altar and called its name,
The-Lord-Is-My-Banner.
—Exodus 17:15 NKJV

Friends in Atlanta established a prayer altar in their home: a table that holds a Bible and candles. They gather around that altar once a week with their three children and share Scripture and prayers. Sometimes they sing during this time they take to remember God.

Altars in the Bible were erected when God showed Himself mighty and faithful on behalf of His people. Jehovah Nissi means "The Lord is my Banner." It was the altar erected by Moses when God gave the Israelites victory over the Amalekites. Moses stood on the hill while Joshua and soldiers fought down in the valley, but the battle was really fought by the Lord.

When I need victory for my battles, God fights for me, because in my own strength I can do nothing. The Lord is my victory Banner.

—Penne

Lord, when I am in a battle, fight for me. Amen.

nurture

I am the good shepherd. The good shepherd gives
His life for the sheep.
—John 10:11 NKJV

N
either my father nor my stepfather knew how to nurture.
Daddy spent more of his time in bars than at home. Joe
ruled the family with rage and unreasonable demands.
I often tried to compensate for my insecurities by eating sweets
(my childish idea of a reward for good behavior) or talking too
much (attention, please?). It took decades to finally believe that
God sees me and doesn't lose His temper when I act human.
One picture of Him that I cling to is found in John 10. God is
my nurturing shepherd. I'm a needy lamb, sometimes wandering off the path and making unwise choices. The shepherd
never scolds or shames. Instead, He finds me and brings me
back to healing and strength. I can rest in His love, a perfect
love from the perfect Father's heart.

—Jeanette

*Thank You, Lord, for nurturing all of Your children
as the Good Shepherd. Amen.*

when

When you go through deep waters, I will be with you.
—Isaiah 43:2 NLT

When I was a boy, I was often frustrated by my parents' most common answers to my questions. "When can I get a bike for my birthday?" "When will we get there?" "When can I go outside?" The typical answer: "Soon." So unsatisfying.

I still ask a lot of questions, though now I direct them to God: "When will I get better at this?" "When will my prayer be answered?" "When will this trial end?" The answer is still, sometimes, "Soon." But most importantly, I know God is with me in every "when." He says: "When you go through deep waters, I will be with you. When you go through rivers of difficulty, you will not drown. When you walk through the fire of oppression, you will not be burned up; the flames will not consume you" (Isa. 43:2–3 NLT).

—Bob

Father, "soon" is soon enough for me—as long as You are with me. Amen.

release

You will cast all our sins into the depths of the sea.
—Micah 7:19 ESV

My neighborhood pond is stocked with fish for recreational anglers to enjoy. The fishing is "catch and release" only, so any fish I'm lucky enough to land must be returned to the pond alive. This way of fishing doesn't put food on my table, but it is instructive for my faith. God doesn't want me to cast my rod into His sea of forgiveness and go fishing for my old transgressions. But against His better advice, I sometimes do it anyway, revisiting and dwelling on my regrets. When I "catch" one, I want to release it quickly back into the waters of forgiveness, trusting that God no longer holds it against me.

—Kirsten

Jesus, I'm sorry for the times I revisit the wrongs for which You've forgiven me. Please help me to release them back into the waters of Your forgiveness. Amen.

go

The Lord had said to Abram, "Go from your country, your people and your father's household to the land I will show you."
—Genesis 12:1 NIV

I have a cautious nature. I don't like to make mistakes. Change doesn't thrill me. I prefer to dip my toe in the pool instead of jumping in. I like to think, mull over, and ruminate. In a perfect world, I'd like to have everything figured out before I take the first step. But life isn't like that.

I've grown to realize that life is about going and doing, not sitting, thinking…and worrying. I simply have to *go*. The word *go* appears in *Strong's Concordance* 1,497 times. God and Jesus repeatedly tell us to *go*! *Go* and live. *Go* and love. *Go* and help. *Go* and share His Word. He wants me to *go*! When God told Abram to go, he went—even though Abram didn't know where he was going. I just love that.

—Janet

Lord, help me to go and do as You please. Amen.

see

Judgments prevent us from seeing the good
that lies beyond appearances.
—Wayne Dyer

I think we humans see more than we used to. I mean, TV, Internet, social media, streaming…that's a lot. But are we really seeing? Social media is the land of the staged, filtered shot. Whether it's dinner or family vacation photos, we only see the surface. We don't see the messy kitchen that produced the meal or the fight moments before about the too-expensive hotel. We see the 24/7 edited news but can't be sure it represents reality. We see the beautiful fashion model but not the hours in makeup or hair or in the postproduction photo-editing.

Really seeing is much harder today. We're saturated by digital images, but we don't take the time to evaluate what we see, to ask God for wisdom to see others, ourselves, and the world clearly. Seeing with God's eyes is a game changer in this troubled world.

—Isabella

Jesus, help me see everything with Your eyes. Amen.

roam

Whether you turn to the right or to the left, your ears will hear
a voice behind you, saying, "This is the way; walk in it."
—Isaiah 30:21 NIV

B rett walked fast and talked faster. His job was to train me
to lead tours in Toronto, and my job was to keep up. He
pointed out historical sites, architecture, shopping areas,
good restaurants, bad restaurants, popular parks, and local
culture. Suddenly he stopped on a congested street corner and
quizzed me: "Which direction is your hotel from here?" Panic
flooded my chest. I had no idea; we had roamed for hours.

In life I like to roam—to try my hand at different careers, to
pursue goals that I only dream of reaching, to experience new
destinations and adventures. I'm thankful that God is with me in
unfamiliar places, giving me turn-by-turn directions and assurance that I'm on the right route.

—Becky

*God, I'm listening for Your voice. Thank You
for guiding me as I roam. Amen.*

defend

Defend my cause and redeem me; preserve my life
according to your promise.
—Psalm 119:154 NIV

One of my earliest memories was formed on the corner
outside my house. I don't remember all the details,
such as what led to the incident or how many bullies
gathered around me. But I do remember my brother Larry,
four-and-a-half years older than I was, sauntering up to the
group, identifying himself as my brother, and letting everyone
know that he wouldn't let harm come to me. We had our differences, like all siblings do, but he was my defender that day.

I still need a defender, as do others around me. So I pray.
I ask Him to defend me when I feel misunderstood. I ask Him
to defend my family against disease and disaster. I ask Him to
defend my church and community, my neighbors and nation,
as well as "the weak and the fatherless…the poor and the
oppressed" (Ps. 82:3 NIV).

—Bob

God, defend all who need it today. Amen.

forbearance

Forbearance is the quality of someone who is patient and able to deal with a difficult person or situation without becoming angry.
—*Merriam-Webster's Learners Dictionary*

Early in my career I had a quarrelsome coworker at my office. Unfortunately, the definition above does not describe how I treated the man. There's no sugarcoating it. I was wrong. But God took hold of my heart, and a colleague took hold of my hand, pulled me aside, and asked, "Why are you being so mean? He's going through a difficult time." My heart broke—my coworker *was* making my life impossible, but it was only because he was broken. God called me to love my coworker, to be patient with him, not fight against him, just as God shows mercy and is patient with me.

—Didi

Lord Jesus, bless me with forbearance, a fruit of the Spirit (Gal. 5:22 NIV). Show me how to exhibit patience with others. Amen.

manna

Then the LORD said to Moses, "I will rain down bread from heaven for you. The people are to go out each day and gather enough for that day."
—Exodus 16:4 NIV

For forty years, God provided manna for the children of Israel as they wandered in the desert. Every morning. He commanded that they take as much as they needed for the day, but no more—any extra for the next day would become rotten and full of maggots.

If I'd been an Israelite, I'm pretty sure I would've tried to sneak a little extra manna, and my plan would have failed.

God has a habit of giving us what we need when we need it, but He usually doesn't pad our spiritual savings accounts with a little extra to keep us from fretting. He wants to build our faith, and that means no safety net, no plan B. Just God.

—Michelle

Dear God, help me to remember that You are always enough. Amen.

pedal

Life is like riding a bicycle. You don't fall off
unless you stop pedaling.
—Claude Pepper

I stood at the top of a grassy slope, my left hand steadying the bicycle's handlebars, my right on the back of the seat. My four-year-old granddaughter June and I locked eyes. "I'm going to run alongside you," I told her. "Look straight ahead. And whatever you do…"

June finished the sentence. "Don't stop pedaling!" Six times, she rested her feet on the pedals but never pushed them. Six times, she fell over. But she always got back on the bike. "Remember the rules," I said.

On the seventh try, June began to pedal. She rode her little pink bike down that grassy slope like a pro. She's been riding like a pro ever since. I pray she'll always take the lessons from that day to heart, and not just when riding a bike.

—Jennie

*Lord, when life's challenges seem to overwhelm me, remind
me to look straight ahead and keep pedaling. Amen.*

retrospect

You can't go back and change the beginning, but you can start where you are and change the ending.
—C.S. Lewis

Retrospect. The word means: *A review or meditation on past events. To reflect.* I tend to look back—a lot. I think of moments in my life I wish I could change. Moments I wish I'd been braver. What if I'd spoken up? What if I'd taken a chance and reached out? There are lots of what-ifs, and it's easy to slip into a rabbit hole, but before I'm in too deep, I rely on a thought that pulls me back out: I can't change the past, but I can learn from it. Instead of dwelling on what happened, it's valuable to look back in retrospect and ponder my actions and decisions, so I can do better next time.

—Sabrina

Thank You, Lord, for reminding me that although I cannot change my past, I can change my future. Amen.

wings

So God created...every winged bird according to its kind.
—Genesis 1:21 NKJV

I hear them before I see them, and I look up, up, up, always surprised that any winged creature can fly two miles above the earth. It's November, and thousands of sandhill cranes are making their way from their summer home up north to spend winter at the Hiwassee Wildlife Refuge near Chattanooga, Tennessee. Their flight path is directly over my neighborhood and, though I witness this migration every year, I never lose my sense of wonder as these magnificent creatures undertake this magnificent journey.

Early in January, I'll visit them while they're on the ground at Hiwassee. I'll gape at their four-foot height and six-foot wingspan. I'll marvel at their lovely gray feathers and bright-red crowns. These cranes are the oldest-known bird species on earth, hunted nearly to extinction by 1900, but—thanks to tireless conservation efforts—are now the most numerous crane species in the world.

—Jennie

How wonderful is Your creation, Lord. Amen.

wait

And sure enough, even waiting will end...
if you can just wait long enough.
—William Faulkner

'm old enough to remember the first office computer. The amount of waiting involved to process information or print— Oh, my! Today, many of us cannot wait to get the latest phone or laptop because the old one is so slow. Used to be, if I wanted to buy something, I'd have to save the money, then tote myself to a store to find what I wanted, or order it from a catalog, which usually involved a wait. Today, instant credit and Amazon Prime enables me to order just about anything and get it that very day. I don't have to wait for movies, books, or answers to many questions.

I, however, am utterly convinced in the power of waiting and so I make it an intentional practice, pausing often, talking to God. Waiting is powerful.

—Isabella

Dad, help me to wait gracefully and consult You in the meantime.
Amen.

trust

All I have seen teaches me to trust the creator
for all I have not seen.
—Ralph Waldo Emerson

I'm an optimist by nature, but still I struggle with worry and doubts. Will I have enough money for retirement? How will I get all my work done and still have time for family? Will my children find decent jobs and be able to live independently? If only I could be sure.

Recently, we spent an afternoon, as a family, reviewing photos we'd taken over the past ten years. There on the TV screen were joyous birthday celebrations, day trips, vacations, high school graduations. So many good times, literally more than I could remember. But something was missing—all the times I'd spent worrying! It turns out, worry hadn't benefited my life one bit. I don't know what the future holds for me, but I can trust that God will be there to see me through.

—Evan

Lord, help me to trust not in myself, but in You. Amen.

run

Even youths grow tired and weary, and young men stumble
and fall; but those who hope in the Lord will renew their
strength. They will soar on wings like eagles; they will run and
not grow weary, they will walk and not be faint.
—Isaiah 40:30–31 NIV

My college mentor, Gayle, was the best. Tall, athletic, and funny. I wanted to be like her. When she signed up for a 10K, I joined her. *How hard could it be?* Apparently, really hard. As I jogged the hilly roads, my lungs screamed for air and my feet hurt. I only finished because of Gayle's encouragement.

Now, I'm running a different race. The one Jesus has set before me. My ability to run is anchored in the hope of His power, grace, and forgiveness. He is the best. I want to be like Him. And because of Him, I will run until the finish.

—Susanna

*Jesus, thank You for Your strength and hope
as I run Your race. Amen.*

strength

The joy of the LORD is your strength.
—Nehemiah 8:10 NKJV

When I'm worn out, at my wit's end, swirling around in a whirlwind of activities and deadlines, I try to stop and focus, so I can regain the strength I need to meet the challenges for that day. I pray silently: "He is with me. He loves me. He is faithful." I find that these and numerous other promises from God's Word fuel my inner strength.

I'm not suggesting that merely repeating these words as positive affirmations will create some new source of mental power in me. But over time, I've located the place in my heart where the experiences and memories of God's presence, love, and faithfulness dwell. That place is a treasure trove of strength.

—Janet

Thank You, dear Lord, for being my strength and my joy. Amen.

bounce

The difference between a strong man and a weak one is that the former does not give up after defeat.
—Woodrow Wilson

I t was heartbreaking to watch my firstborn come home in tears after being left out at recess that day. I stayed calm, then later vented to a friend that I never wanted my daughter to feel hurt. My friend countered, "She's going to feel hurt someday. Wouldn't you rather be present to help her process it?" That's when my purpose as a parent was really clarified. I couldn't keep my kids from harm, but I could help them wade through and make sense of their feelings when something happened. The next day, I woke up ready to listen and provide guidance. Most of all, we talked about how important it is to bounce back, with kindness, and meet the coming day.

—Ashley

Lord, help me put aside hurt for a chance at renewal and learn how best to move forward. Amen.

justice

The way to right wrongs is to turn the light
of truth upon them.
—Ida B. Wells

I didn't know how close I'd come to being benched until after the situation was addressed and resolved. I was relieved, but also concerned because of what almost happened. Our soccer team's new head coach thought I was coasting and not giving one hundred percent during practice, something he thought was unacceptable, The head coach shared his disciplinary plan with our assistant head coach, who explained the issue was really a cultural difference. The head coach was from Europe and the team was from the US. The assistant coach was able to verify that after years of working with me, I was indeed exerting maximum effort. Justice prevailed. My position and standing on the team remained intact because the assistant coach came to my defense, righted a perceived wrong, and acted as a bridge of understanding.

—Steve

*Lord, help me choose to be a bridge of understanding,
especially when justice is at risk. Amen.*

therefore

We having the same spirit of faith, according as it is written, I believed, and therefore have I spoken; we also believe, and therefore speak...
—2 Corinthians 4:13 KJV

Years ago, God gave me a vision for a women's ministry. It started out as an idea to empower women to dream and pursue their God-given purpose. In my mind's eye I could see it. I could visualize women getting healed and set free from what I call "dream killers": negative thoughts or beliefs that hold us back.

Almost from the beginning I had faith that the Dream Girls ministry would come to pass.

I started to talk about it, and then I started to plan and build Dream Girls. I believed, and therefore I spoke!

Therefore is a conjunctive adverb that connects two thoughts. In the Scripture above it connects what we believe with what we speak. When we believe with all our heart, we therefore speak. Never underestimate the power of *therefore*!

—Penne

Lord, help me to believe, and therefore speak. Amen.

empathy

Empathy is...emotionally connecting, and communicating that incredibly healing message of "You're not alone."
—Brene Brown

I was ten when my fun-loving daddy died of cirrhosis of the liver. Throughout my teen years, I asked God "why?" a thousand times. Why did my dad fill my life with laughter and then leave me after such a short time? As an adult, I lamented that my heart was too sensitive to others' pain. I had to cover my ears and leave the room if someone mentioned child or animal abuse. When a friend's wife died suddenly, I felt his grief as if it were mine.

God recently showed me that my tender heart was a result of losing Daddy. And He had replaced that Daddy-shaped hole in my soul with empathy for anyone who hurts. The Lord didn't cause Daddy's death. But He used it to create my caring heart.
—Jeanette

Thank You, Lord, for using life's painful times to produce empathy in me. Amen.

smile

When I smiled at them, they scarcely believed it;
the light of my face was precious to them.
—Job 29:24 NIV

I looked in the mirror…more wrinkles than I had time to count. And when did that double chin show up? I longed for my face to match my feelings—those of a thirty-year-old ready to change the world. But thanks to God's grace, encouragement from wise friends, and a couple books about positive thinking, my emotions were in their best shape ever. That thought birthed a smile. A huge smile that flooded my heart with joy and contentment. I'm sure a psychologist can explain why smiling lifts our spirits and improves our mood. I really don't care. Because when I looked in the mirror a second time, those wrinkles and extra chin had lost their hold on me.

—Jeanette

*Please help me, Lord, to welcome thoughts that make
me smile. When I smile, I feel Your love. Amen.*

how

"How will this be," Mary asked the angel.
—Luke 1:34 NIV

When my wife and I moved into a new home not long ago, we "inherited" from the previous owner a satellite dish mounted on the side of our house. I wanted to remove it but couldn't figure out how (without damaging something—or someone). I called on a neighbor to think through it with me. We bounced a few thoughts off of each other, eventually came up with a plan, and it worked.

When the angel appeared to Mary to tell her that she had been chosen to give birth to the long-awaited Messiah, she asked, "How will this be?" The angel answered, in effect, that it would involve a partnership—of submission on her part and power on God's part. That's pretty much how anything challenging gets done in my world. For me, praying "How?" isn't so much a plea for information as for partnership.

—Bob

Lord, show me how to meet the challenge of this day. Amen.

green

Do not be afraid, you wild animals, for the pastures in the wilderness are becoming green. The trees are bearing their fruit; the fig tree and the vine yield their riches.
—Joel 2:22 NIV

According to "The Ballad of Davy Crockett," I live in the greenest state in the land of the free—Tennessee. Yet sometimes I fear that our lushness is disappearing. It doesn't snow in winter like it used to. Summer comes early and stays too long. Rain is often scarce. Those same things are happening all over our planet.

I worry.

But I also act in whatever ways I can to help keep the earth green. Recycle. Avoid single-use plastic. Pick up litter. Drive less. Put the poisons aside. Collect water in a rain barrel. Dry laundry on a clothesline. Vote for candidates pledged to care for the environment.

I like to think I'm making ole Davy proud.

—Jennie

Help us, O Lord, to be good stewards of this amazing home You've given us. Amen.

reflect

In a mirror is where we find a reflection of our appearances, but in our heart is where we find the reflection of our soul.
—Unknown

I don't like to look at myself in a mirror. Inevitably I see only the things I don't like—a too big nose, tired eyes, a sturdy body, and many other perceived imperfections. Maybe I need to look in the mirror and reflect on the unique me that God created. A large mouth that allows me to smile big. Two strong arms that let me give others big hugs. Two legs that take me to explore the wonders of the earth. And my hands are perfect for digging in the garden, cooking for my family, helping others in need.

Next time I look in a mirror, I'll be happy with my reflection because that's the me God created.

—Carolyn

Thank You, God, for my physical gifts. Help me to embrace who You made me to be. Amen.

season

To everything there is a season, a time for
every purpose under heaven.
—Ecclesiastes 3:1 NKJV

I walked out of the air-conditioned supermarket into the scorching August afternoon. Heat waves shimmered off the pavement as I pushed my buggy through the parking lot. "Whew!" I said, louder than I meant to.

The woman loading groceries into the trunk of the car next to me smiled. "Come January," she said, "you'll be wishing for this."

Fast forward to January, one of the coldest on record. *Gosh, I found myself thinking as I walked the dog early one frigid morning. I sure wish summer would get here.* Yikes. I thought back to the August conversation in the supermarket parking lot. Clearly, I hadn't taken its lesson to heart. Seasons change. Summer becomes autumn becomes winter becomes spring. Shivers become sweat. Sweat becomes shivers. It's part of God's grand design. And it's brilliant.

—Jennie

Heavenly Father, may I be ever mindful that every season has its beauty and its purpose. Amen.

moon

I see the moon, the moon sees me.
The moon sees somebody I'd like to see.
—Children's lullaby

've always been mesmerized by the moon, whether a pale, crescent "fingernail" moon or a gigantic full moon, round and orange as a basketball, rising in the east just as the sun sets in the west. My daddy sang me the "I See the Moon" lullaby when I was little, and it's been one of my favorite songs ever since. He told me that when he was a soldier in Korea, he'd look up at the moon and know that seven thousand miles away in Arkansas, the very same moon was shining down on my mother.

Whenever I start missing someone who lives far away or, especially, my beloved parents who reside now with our Heavenly Father, I take comfort in knowing we're all looking up at the same beautiful moon.

—Jennie

God bless the moon and God bless me. God bless the
somebody I'd like to see. Amen.

guide

Guide me, O Thou great Jehovah.
—William Williams

My daughter had saved up and was ready to buy her own car. But the car she wanted was equipped with manual transmission, and she had never driven a car with a stick shift. So, on the test drive, she sat in the driver's seat and, when the time came to change gears, she pressed the clutch and put her hand on the gearshift. I then put my hand over hers and moved the lever. After a few times through the process, she was ready to do it herself, while I watched. She bought the car.

I pray often for God to do that sort of thing for me, especially when I'm facing a new challenge. Wherever I go, whatever I do, I want to say, "even there your hand will guide me, your right hand will hold me fast" (Ps. 139:10 NIV).

—Bob

God, guide me with Your powerful hand today. Amen.

tradition

Tradition lives because young people come along who
catch its romance and add new glories to it.
—Michael Novak

My family has lots of traditions. The best ones?
Spending holidays together. Thanksgiving and
Christmas are the two holidays when I know I'll see a
lot of family, and it's a treat. And very important to all of us. One
Thanksgiving, when my uncle asked us what we were thankful
for, I said it was the ability to come together every year, while
many other families may not. My uncle reminded us of the
importance of this tradition, pointing out that for generations,
our family always made sure to spend the Thanksgiving and
Christmas holidays together. He then looked at the younger
generation and made us *promise* to keep this tradition alive
even after all our elders are gone. To me, that was an easy
promise to make. There's nothing else I'd rather do.

—Sabrina

Thank You, Lord, for letting me see the positives in traditions.
Amen.

others

We rise by lifting others.
—Robert Ingersoll

I go to church every Sunday. Rain or shine, sleet or snow. Sometimes the sermons really speak to me, and sometimes they don't. Sometimes the biblical lesson feels applicable, and sometimes I can't make any sense of it. Sometimes I like the music we're singing, and sometimes I don't. But that's not why I'm there.

Many years ago, the Salvation Army was looking for a word—one word—they could telegraph to say what they were about. The word? *Others.* I show up at church for *others,* the community of the faithful, and together we rise.

—Rick

Dear Lord, thank You for giving me a faith community to guide and support me week after week. Let me be steadfast in my love for others as You love me, day in, day out. Amen.

written

And the LORD answered me: "Write the vision; make it
plain on tablets, so he may run who reads it."
—Habakkuk 2:2 ESV

I cherish handwritten notes from loved ones, as well as my own notes. In class, while taking notes, I would scribble my favorite song lyrics, or whatever phrase was stuck in my head that day. A few weeks ago, I wrote down what I wanted for my future. The list included things like traveling to various places with friends and family, buying my dream house, marrying, having kids, and other goals and dreams. Although I typically thought about and prayed for these things daily, writing them down made my intentions clear for what I wanted in my life. Sharing these written goals and dreams with others leaves them available to help me fulfill them, and I'm open to all the help I can get.

—Jaylin

Lord, please help me fulfill my written dreams. Amen.

seed

Everything that exists is in a manner the seed of that which will be.
—Marcus Aurelius

'm not much of a green thumb, but I've learned a lot because I enjoy pretty flowers and homegrown herbs. But only recently did I get another glimpse into God's ways. I never much thought about seeds until I planted some wildflowers. I followed the instructions, tilling the soil, covering the seeds gently, and watering regularly. When you plant seeds, it seems like forever before you see anything. Then one day the most fragile wisp of a seedling poked through the dirt, then another, then another. Once out, they grew quickly. I realized there's a lot going on in the damp darkness before I ever see a sprout. It's that invisible work that produces what becomes a beautiful flower, a fragrant herb, or good food.

—Isabella

God, help me trust what You're doing in the darkness and trust I, too, will be fruitful if I lovingly tend my spirit. Amen.

mirror

Let us be grateful to the mirror for revealing
to us our appearance only.
—Samuel Butler

When I scroll through photographs on my phone, I'm sometimes startled by the face smiling back at me. The mental image I carry of myself doesn't include the graying hair or aging skin the images reveal; I forget that I actually look my age. In those moments, I feel a little like the kind of person James describes who "immediately forgets what he looks like" after looking in a mirror (James 1:24 NIV).

God's Word is the mirror that shows me the true condition of my heart instead of my face. I may not always like what the mirror of His Word reveals to me about myself, but it reminds me of Jesus's remedy for my wrongdoings and gives me the opportunity to instead do what God desires. James says we'll be blessed when we do.

—Kirsten

Thank You, Lord, for showing me how to live in a way that pleases You. Amen.

wag

Wag more. Bark less.
—Sign in a pet store window

Though I'm not a regular volunteer, I occasionally visit my local animal shelter to play with the dogs. When I enter the canine dorm, the barks are deafening. "ME FIRST! ME FIRST!" many of the dogs implore. I saunter past the row of cages until I find a quiet dog. I stop in front of his cage. Invariably, he wags his tail. That's the dog I pick. If time allows, I play with all of them. But waggers always take priority over barkers.

That's how I chose the dog I recently adopted. Kamala was sitting calmly in her pen and looking straight into my eyes. When the door opened, she flew into my arms. She has floppy ears, soft fur, a compact, muscular body, and a tail so strong it can clear a coffee table. A tail that's always wagging.

—Jennie

Remind me, Lord, to choose joy over noise. Just like my dog does. Amen.

rock

Trust in the LORD forever, for the LORD, the LORD himself,
is the Rock eternal.
—Isaiah 26:4 NIV

When I was younger, I collected rocks. I was fascinated by them. I arranged them however I wanted, I threw them into rivers, or I took them home as keepsakes. Then I learned about another type of rock that I could not manipulate: a mountain. The number of hikers, campers, or explorers that scale it doesn't matter, nor do the boisterous winds or torrential rains that assail it. The foundation of this type of rock can't be manipulated by man. It's fixed. Which is just how fixed Jesus is in my life when I make Him my Rock. People come and go in my life, but God remains forever strong, stable, and secure. From collecting rocks to standing on the Rock, God is forever my strength.

—Ty'Ann

*Lord, thank You that You are my Lord, my Rock forever.
I trust in You. Amen.*

river

Love is the river of life in the world.
—Henry Ward Beecher

We have an irrigation canal that runs behind the back of our house. It is one of many that services the farming community surrounding our home. I love walking along its banks, and I am not the only one. Birds flock to it. Geese patrol its banks. My son, Addison, has even spotted a fox and its kit nearby.

Why do we all love rushing waters? Since creation, rivers have ushered in life and growth. Without rivers, animals, crops, and cities perish.

Just like our farming community needs the canal's constant supply of water, I need the river of God's love flowing constantly through my life. Tributaries of hope. Rivulets of grace. Streams of peace. Without His Spirit constantly moving through my life, I would perish. His river of love quenches my parched soul. His river is life-giving.

—Susanna

God, flood my life with Your river of love. Amen.

who

I need to listen, listen for the prayer of God that is rising in my heart, perhaps for the prayer that I should be praying rather than the one that I am praying.

—Robert Benson

L ike many people, I maintain a list of people for whom I'm praying. Some (my wife, children, grandchildren, etc.) I pray for every day—even multiple times each day. Others I pray for intermittently.

Sometimes, however, I ask God who *He* wants me to pray for. I'll try to clear my mind, and say simply, "Who?" Sometimes a name—or several—will come to mind almost immediately. Sometimes I sit in silence for a minute or two before my question is answered. Sometimes a person enters my thoughts who could only have been suggested by God, someone I don't know or haven't thought of in years. But I pray, believing that God has answered my "Who?" prayer.

—Bob

Father, whom shall I pray for today? Amen.

chance

A wise man turns chance into good fortune.
—Thomas Fuller

Growing up, I was always the cautious one. If there was a curfew, I kept it. A deadline, I met it. So, when I graduated from college and realized that my perfectly planned life wasn't going according to plan, I felt lost. My sister called me and said, "Just come here. Take a chance on something different!" I left New Jersey and headed to North Carolina for six months of random adventures and new experiences I never dreamed could happen. At the end of my time in North Carolina, my job-related dreams did come true. I'm incredibly happy with my well-planned life now, but those six months of uncharted bliss were the ones that laid the groundwork for my being ready for what came next.

—Ashley

*Thank You, God, for showing up in my uncertainty
and giving me the chance to fly free. Amen.*

path

You make known to me the path of life;
you will fill me with joy in your presence.
—Psalm 16:11 NIV

I was lost. Unfortunately, I was also the one who was supposed to know where we were going. Four a.m., pitch black...ugh. I had several hikers behind me, all of them eager to climb the famous Snake Trail up the mountain to Israel's Masada Fortress and to watch a spectacular Dead Sea sunrise. Except our trail didn't take us up to Masada. It terminated at an equipment shed. I looked at the building in the flashlight beam and sighed.

I'd like to say that little mishap was the only wrong trail I've taken in life. But...let's just say I've visited a lot of equipment sheds. I'm so glad the real Trail Guide has a long history of stepping in. His flashlight is so much brighter, His sense of direction infallible.

Even that dark morning.

The sunrise was spectacular.

—Buck

Thank You for Your never-ending patience with me. Amen.

gift

And in their prayers for you their hearts will go out to you...
Thanks be to God for his indescribable gift!
—2 Corinthians 9:14–15 NIV

M rs. Shrum, a veteran teacher, taught next door to an inexperienced, overwhelmed first-year teacher. Me. Every morning she had a cup of coffee and a word of encouragement. One day I gave her a thank-you gift, a new coffee cup, for being a wonderful mentor. She said, "I'll pray for you every time I drink from this." Later, I found out that all her coffee cups had been gifts! She started each morning by praying for the person who had given her the cup she would drink from that day. Twenty-five years later, as I pour my morning coffee, I pray for the special someone who gave me the cup I'm filling. I gave Mrs. Shrum a gift of appreciation, but what a gift she gave me in return!

—Karen

Father, thank You for praying friends.
What an indescribable gift they are. Amen.

rest

Come to Me, all you who labor and are heavy laden,
and I will give you rest. Take My yoke upon you
and learn from Me...you will find rest for your souls.
—Matthew 11:28–30 NKJV

When my dear pastor friend, Dr. Churn, encouraged me in prayer to "rest, and nest, in Him," my ears perked up, my shoulders lowered, and my whole body started to take a much-needed breath. The phrase she spoke remains with me.

Rest doesn't come easily to me; there's always something to do, someone to help, or a conversation to be had. Yet Jesus wants me to find time to rest: to remain connected to Him, to rest in and "learn" from Him. The simple plea in the Scripture above to come and rest is actually a priceless gift, an invitation to lay down my cares, tune out the world, and rest, and nest, in Him.

—Janet

*Today, Lord, help me remember the oceans of peace
and relaxation available as I rest in You. Amen.*

sacrifice

True love is sacrifice. It is in giving, not in getting; in losing, not in gaining; in realizing, not in possessing, that we love.
—Quoteistan.com

Our granddaughter Jenessa turned seventeen last year. My husband, Kevin, and I offered to treat her to dinner at any restaurant she chose—within reason. After our casual Chinese meal, Jenessa wanted dessert at a frozen yogurt/ice cream shop. Kevin isn't a fan of yogurt. Nor could he hide his disappointment over the choices of ice cream flavors. "Let's go somewhere everyone likes," Jenessa said. No matter how much Kevin argued that it was her birthday, we should eat where she chose, and he didn't need dessert anyway, Jenessa persisted. We ended up at a delightful pie shop. I was proud of both my loved ones—especially our mature young lady—for their sweet sacrifice.

—Jeanette

Lord, please give me a heart that's willing to sacrifice my wishes for another's benefit. Amen.

discipline

Discipline is just choosing between what you want
now and what you want most.
—Abraham Lincoln

My college buddies really wanted me to hang out with
them, but I had an early job interview the next morning. Staying out late didn't seem like a big deal to
them, but I needed to be fresh and alert for the one-hour drive.
There had been lots of nights out with friends over the years,
but graduation was just around the corner, so they kept up the
pressure. I took a few minutes to think and realized that after
four years, my buddies and I had established the foundation for
a lifetime of friendship.

I decided not to socialize that night. Commitment to my
future meant a small degree of sacrifice in the present. At
age twenty-one, I was learning and applying the principle of
discipline that would serve me often, and well, throughout my
adult life.

—Steve

*Lord, please help me to always practice discipline, and remember
that future gains are worth sacrifices now. Amen.*

perseverance

I am your God; I will strengthen you, I will help you,
I will uphold you with my righteous right hand.
—Isaiah 41:10 ESV

My daughter, Zoe, has always been wise beyond her years. Even as a toddler, she would occasionally admonish me: "*Are you sure you should be letting me do* [insert questionable parenting choice]?"

When Zoe was six, I committed to a rigorous 5:00 a.m. workout routine. Zoe, an early riser, would frequently join me. But as days passed, I grew tired. Getting up at 5:00 a.m. was tough.

One morning, after hitting the snooze button, I decided to sleep in and not work out. Then Zoe's small face appeared in front of mine. "*Dad, are you showing perseverance?*" Getting called out by a six-year-old will get you out of bed quickly!

Many times I've wanted to give up when things got hard, but I'm grateful God puts reminders everywhere to persevere.

—John

*Dear Lord, strengthen me to persevere. Remind me that,
through You, all things are possible. Amen.*

happy

This is the day the Eternal God has made; let us
celebrate and be happy today.
—Psalm 118:24 VOICE

When I was in my twenties, I attended dozens of weddings. I was happy for my friends, and I hoped that one day soon I'd be the bride. My thirties came and went. While I had a very good life and appreciated it, I believed that I wouldn't *really* be happy until—or unless—I was married. I had it wrong on so many levels! God says, "Be happy *today*."

I now know that I don't have to wait until all of my bills are paid or I get a clean bill of health in order to be happy. The psalmist reminds me that *this* is the day that God has given me, and because of that alone, I can be happy.

—Michelle

Dear Father, thank You for the blessings You've showered on me.
Help me to focus on them today and to be grateful. Amen.

protect

He will cover you with his feathers, and under
his wings you will find refuge; his faithfulness will be
your shield and rampart.
—Psalm 91:4 NIV

I t was my twenty-fourth birthday and I felt protected. That year I got to know God as Mighty, Holy, and Wonderful. God had safeguarded me, showing Himself strong in a multitude of ways.

The year before I'd left a difficult home environment, and now I was in a place that was very different than what I had experienced for nearly two years. During that time, my mentally unstable uncle starting leaving the front door of my home wide open—for months on end. I used to imagine the multitude of scenarios that could have happened to me, but because of God's protection, nothing bad ever did.

—Kiana

Lord, thank You for always protecting me from things seen and unseen. Thank You that You are always my ever-present help. Amen.

diversity

Isn't it amazing that we are all made in God's image, and yet there is so much diversity among his people?
—Archbishop Desmond Tutu

A well-traveled native Californian raised in Maryland, I moved to Florida a few years ago. I still marvel at Florida's exotic beauty. As a global destination, Florida also brims with human diversity—people from every corner of the planet, each person unique. I think I love the Florida Suncoast so much because I see it all as a creative expression of God's heart. He demonstrates His love abundantly everywhere, in all things. In humanity alone, the differences are striking and cellular. To think every single one of us has a unique DNA and thumbprint! That's more than 7.5 billion people! Even so, we share one vital quality that unifies us: Our Creator delights in each one of us equally.

—Isabella

Dad, help me be ever mindful that my natural and human community is entirely created and loved by You. Equally. Amen.

instill

We don't do drugs, drink or use profanity. Instead we instill morals and values in my boys by raising them with a love of God and a love and respect for themselves and all people.
—Anita Baker

I try to drink a lot of water for health reasons. I find that it's easier when I'm drinking something with flavor, so several times a day, I empty a small packet of powdered flavoring into a tall tumbler of water. Often as I do that and stir the water, I pray. I like to pray using mental triggers, and the act of instilling my water with flavor reminds me to pray for biblical virtues and the fruit of God's Spirit to be instilled in my children and grandchildren. I pray for them to grow in grace and to live lives of love. To respect themselves and others. To exercise self-discipline. To be honest, kind, and generous. And so much more.

—Bob

God, instill in those I love the fruit of Your presence. Amen.

lost

"For I know the plans I have for you," declares the LORD,
"plans to prosper you and not to harm you, plans to give
you hope and a future."
—Jeremiah 29:11 NIV

Going to college without a major or a career in mind made me feel lost and out of place. All my new friends seemed to know what career path they wanted. "Maybe I should change schools or take time off and go back home?" I vented to one of my friends.

"Don't go home!" he said, catching me off guard. "Everyone our age feels lost sometimes, and you'll have so many more opportunities at school than in your hometown." His words really stuck with me, and within a few months, I started to find my way. I wasn't lost after all.

—Jaylin

*Lord, thank You for using my mother's favorite
Bible verse to remind me that You have a plan for me. Amen.*

seen

She gave this name to the LORD who spoke to her:
"You are the God who sees me," for she said, "I have
now seen the One who sees me."
—Genesis 16:13 NIV

Have you ever secretly worried you might be invisible? I have. In social settings, I prefer to fly under the radar and engage one-on-one. But at the same time, I need to feel seen and heard. I want to know I matter, make some sort of impact, even to one person.

I remember many social situations in which I've met someone and struck up a memorable conversation, only to have that person not remember me the next time we meet. *Did I make so little impact?*

When I feel that way, I take comfort in knowing that my Heavenly Father always has His eye on me—that He sees my heart, my needs, my insecurities, my longings. I'm *not* invisible; I'm truly seen.

—Jon

God, thank You that with You, I'm seen. I matter to You. Amen.

anointed

The Spirit of the Lord is upon me, because he hath anointed
me to preach the gospel to the poor; he hath sent me
to heal the brokenhearted, to preach deliverance to the
captives, and recovering of sight to the blind, to set
at liberty them that are bruised.
—Luke 4:18 KJV

The phrase "anointed me to preach the gospel to the poor" rings in my ears whenever I read it or hear it. One night while I slept, I heard those words spoken in a dream. When I woke up, I wasn't sure what anointed meant, but over time I came to realize it meant to be equipped with the necessary tools to fulfill the mission. When Jesus was just starting His ministry, He announced He was anointed to preach the gospel. I, too, am anointed to share the gospel with those around me. When we operate in the anointing of God, His Spirit is with us.

—Penne

God, thank You for anointing me to share the gospel. Amen.

begin

If we live in the Spirit, let us also walk in the Spirit.
—Galatians 5:25 KJV

An old Jamaican guy once told me—as he was looking down at an endless hardwood floor we were about to install—"It's not how long it takes, *mon*, it's when you start. Once you do, you're practically done." That was right before he cut his finger off with a power saw, but that's a story for another time. I've found my nine-fingered friend's advice was on the money. It still rings through my brain, all these years later.

Are you a procrastinator like me? I can spend a long time staring at uninstalled floors, even when it's something God has called me to do. The thing is, all He asks of us is to *begin*. When we do, He has a wonderful way of taking care of the rest. Before we know it, we're standing there on His beautiful craftsmanship.

—Buck

Thank You, Jesus, for being the wind at my back. Amen.

friendship

Friendship...is born at the moment when one man says to another, "What! You too? I thought that no one but myself..."
—C.S. Lewis

When my parents ask me why I don't spend a lot of time hanging with friends, I remind them that my friends are few and that they're scattered across the East Coast. Growing up, I had many acquaintances at school. But in college, things changed. I realized who my true friends were, and those treasured friendships are still ones I hold on to today. I have two from childhood, several from college, and newer ones. None of my friends live close by, but it doesn't matter. Our friendships have been solidified by shared experiences, time spent in great conversation, and a real deep desire to stay connected. I'm grateful I can go to each one of my friends and talk about absolutely everything and anything. What a gift.

—Sabrina

Thank You, Lord, for amazing friends who care for me. Amen.

unity

Behold, how good and how pleasant it is
for brethren to dwell together in unity!
—Psalm 133:1 KJV

How would two different groups of people interact and get along on a tour bus in Israel? True, we were all from the US, but we were also from different regions, represented different church denominations with different traditions, and began our journey as total strangers. At first everyone was cautiously polite and cordial, but soon things progressed, and we were switching seats and taking photos together. Lots of photos!

Then something awesome happened on our boat ride on the Sea of Galilee. Tentatively, we taught one another new songs, and that gave way to enthusiastically embracing the other group's cultural traditions and styles. Our voices rose, blending beautifully, and wide smiles invited hugs. Tears of joy and amazement flowed freely at what we were experiencing. In that boat, on that sea, our two groups had become one.

—Steve

Thank You, Lord, for unity, the power and beauty of coming together as one. Amen.

illuminate

Judging others makes us blind, whereas love is illuminating.
—Dietrich Bonhoeffer

I have special blackout shades on my bedroom windows so I can sleep at night. The faintest glimmer of light can bring me out of a dead sleep. The only problem is that I have incredibly poor night vision. When I walk around the room with the lights off and the blinds closed, I end up bruising my shins and stubbing my toes. In the dark, I am a poor judge of how things really stand. Light brings clarity. Jesus's love is the light that illuminates my life. I need that love to show me how to navigate the rough edges of the world, to reveal the truth of who people are, and to light the path that Jesus wants me to take. Without the illumination of His divine love, I stumble around in the dark.
—Susanna

Jesus, illuminate my heart with Your love. Bring clarity and hope to the darkness of my soul. Amen.

moment

Rejoice in the things that are present; all else is beyond thee.
—Michel de Montaigne

've often written about the overwhelming time after my son, Isaac, was born with Down syndrome. I was crushed with consuming grief, fear, and dread that nearly leveled me. Caring lovingly for Isaac moment to moment saved me. Sometimes I would repeat aloud, "I'm changing a diaper" or "I'm driving the car" over and over to rein in my thoughts to the present. Before too long, the worried wondering fell away, and I learned to entrust an unknown future to God.

Today, I'm free to fully enjoy the awesome gift that is Isaac. I'm still learning from Isaac how to live my life fully in the moment, something Isaac does so very well. I've come to believe it's one reason Isaac enjoys life so very much.

—Isabella

Daddy, please help me remain squarely in the moment with You, always trusting that You'll provide everything I need. Amen.

leap

Without leaps of imagination or dreaming,
we lose the excitement of possibilities.
—Gloria Steinem

'm going to Italy to take a painting class," my best friend
from high school said after graduation. "Want to come?"
I'm a planner. I know what I want, set expectations, and
meet them, so when the opportunity arose to go on a six-week
detour, I couldn't imagine why I *would* go. But my mom said,
"Go! Don't just watch the parade; join it." Those six weeks in
Italy were a tiny fraction of my life, but I look back with awe that
I took a leap and tried something new. Now when I think of
myself as the predictable girl with three kids, a dog, a job, and
a happy marriage, I remind myself I'm also the girl who took
a leap, went to Italy, and learned to paint landscapes from an
instructor named Roberto.

—Ashley

*Lord, thank You for security and fanciful whims. Lead me
to seek a balance according to Your will. Amen.*

bless

The LORD bless you and keep you.
—Numbers 6:24 NIV

A friend recently told me that his son and daughter-in-law began a tradition with their firstborn. They hung over the boy's bed a framed representation of the Aaronic blessing from the Bible: "The Lord bless you and keep you; the Lord make His face shine on you and be gracious to you; the Lord turn His face toward you and give you peace." Each night, as they tucked him into bed, they blessed him with those words. Now, whenever my friend visits, the child asks, "Will you bless me?"

The single word *bless* is a great way to pray—and thoroughly biblical. Pray it for yourself. For your day. And for those around you, for those you meet on your commute, for those you share an office with, for those you pass on the sidewalk, and more.

—Bob

Lord, bless me and all with whom I come in contact today. Amen.

clutter

Instead of thinking I am losing something when
I clear clutter, I dwell on what I might gain.
—Lisa J. Schultz

'm on my hands and knees, digging through a deep corner
cabinet in my kitchen, searching for an angel food cake pan. I
know it's among the clutter collected in the belly of the poorly
designed cabinet—somewhere. As I pull out item after item, I
begin making piles: junk to discard, things for a yard sale, some
to keep. I find the pan that started my impromptu decluttering
mission and reorganize the cabinet with the items I will keep.
Neat and orderly, each piece is visible and my soul feels lighter.
I stand from my kneeling position and consider how cluttered
my brain is: to-do lists, negative news stories, a difficult person
at work. Maybe it's time to declutter my headspace, too, and
make room for only the most important things.

—Karen

*Father, help me recognize the clutter that keeps me
from dwelling on Your goodness. Amen.*

curiosity

Remember to look up at the stars and not down at your feet. Try to make sense of what you see and wonder about what makes the universe exist. Be curious. And however difficult life may seem, there is always something you can do and succeed at.
—Stephen Hawking

The hallmark of my mother's personality was an avid curiosity. She lived in California and we were in New York, but I could count on her asking me tons of questions when we talked on the phone. I'd tell her all about the kids—that good grade, the goal they scored in soccer, or how they finally learned to ride a two-wheeler. Our two sons are grown now and live across the country. When they call, I aim to be filled with curiosity and a good listener, savoring every detail. Like Mom.

—Rick

Lord, I find a helpful model in Your Son's witness, always asking the disciples questions. Give me the curiosity to seek, to know, and to understand. Amen.

pull

And (Samson) pushed with all his might.
—Judges 16:30 NKJV

I was the new girl in school. Alone in the girls' restroom on my first day of first grade, I finished my business and tried to open the stall door. But though I pushed with all my might, the door wouldn't budge. What was I to do? The walls were too high to climb over. The floor was wet and muddy. I sure didn't want to crawl under.

Struggling to hold back tears, I waited. Finally, someone entered the restroom. "Help," I said in a small voice. The stall door swung toward me and there stood my teacher, smiling.

"You pushed when you should have pulled," she said. It's a lesson I've never forgotten, especially when it comes to my relationship with God. He won't let me push Him away, even though I try sometimes. His loving arms never fail to pull me in.

—Jennie

Pull me, Lord, ever closer to You. Amen.

relish

Think big thoughts but relish small pleasures.
—H. Jackson Brown Jr.

It's the day before Thanksgiving, and I stand at my kitchen counter, chopping. I'm taking cranberry relish to tomorrow's celebration. On the cutting board before me are apples and oranges and pecans and celery. Cranberries, too, of course. I could use a food processor to do this, but I won't. I relish the chopping that's required for real homemade relish.

Yeah. Relish is one of those words that's both noun and verb. It's a noun on Thanksgiving and anytime I eat hot dogs. Most other times, it's a verb. One of my favorite verbs. *To take pleasure in*, it means. This morning, with gratitude, I made a list of just a few things I relish. The beauty of the sunrise. The taste of toothpaste. The smell of coffee brewing. The softness of my dog's fur as I snapped on her leash. The song of the birds.

—Jennie

Make me ever grateful, Lord, for the pleasures of life. Amen.

and

Call to me and I will answer you and tell you great
and unsearchable things you do not know.
—Jeremiah 33:3 NIV

The word *and* is my favorite, and the most helpful of all of the conjunctions. *And* is filled with hope; it suggests that there's always more possible, more to come—another opportunity beyond what may have felt like the final chance. *And, and, and...* But sometimes the hopeful "And then..." turns into the fearful, "And then what?" and dread starts to creep in.

But then I remember that I can either let *and* take me down or lift me up. *And* can be used to create something new and better when I invite God to step in and fill in what will happen next. Adding *and* into the mix as I contemplate a sticky situation opens up possibilities and makes room for the new thing He will do.

—Janet

Lord, thank You for giving me life and hope and for always being there when I call. Amen.

stretch

I am interested only in stretching myself,
in living as fully as I can.
—Doris Lessing

Filled with pain after a bitter divorce, I struggled to find my way out of the darkness. A friend suggested a stretch and tone class. "Exercise will do you good. I think you should try it," she said.

The exercise studio was peaceful and lovely, with windows across one wall and floor-to-ceiling mirrors on another. "We'll focus on three things," my teacher said. "How to breathe. How to balance. How to stretch." During that first class, I didn't inhale or exhale at the right time. At one point I fell over. I couldn't even stretch far enough to clasp my hands behind my back. But every time I practiced, I got better. At breathing. At balancing. Most of all, at stretching. Not just stretching my muscles, but also stretching my determination to live a full and happy life.

—Jennie

O God, I stretch out my arms to You. Amen.

fasting

And I set my face unto the LORD God, to seek by prayer and supplications, with fasting, and sackcloth, and ashes.
—Daniel 9:3 KJV

Right after we got married, I joined the church my husband, Emerson, attended. Some years later, we felt led to join another church. Soon after joining our new church, the pastor announced a forty-day fast. I had never fasted for forty days, and I wasn't sure I could do it…

I did make it through the forty-day fast, but it wasn't easy. The fast was supposed to be a sacred time of drawing closer to God through focused prayer and seeking His face. Instead, I was focused on getting through the grueling days without food! God has taught me many lessons since that first fast. Most importantly, I learned to spend uninterrupted time with Him in prayer, seeking His will, and listening for the revelation and wisdom of the Holy Spirit.

—Rosalind

Father, during times of fasting and prayer, help me develop a more intimate relationship with You. Amen.

know

A humble knowledge of thyself is a surer way to God than a
deep search after learning.
—Thomas à Kempis

As a studious sort who likes to read, I know quite a bit
of stuff. History, philosophy, computers, music, crafts,
random trivia—and yes, the Bible and other spiritual
paths. And because I'm a good talker, sometimes people
believe I'm authoritative. I don't deliberately mislead them.
They just think it. Mostly, though, I know just a little bit about a
lot of things. But since I'm a little absentminded, I also forget
a bunch of details. Lately, I've come to realize that it doesn't
really matter that my knowledge is incomplete. Finally there's
one thing I believe I know really well. It's really all that matters.
I know God is love and that He is everything. Everything else
flows from that. To know God and His love is what matters most
of all.

—Isabella

Dear God, open my heart and mind that I might know
You better still. Amen.

weather

Never judge a day by the weather.
—Zig Ziglar

Temperatures dropped quickly as rain began to fall. Soon, layers of ice knocked down power lines across the county. Recently separated from my husband, I was living in a new-to-me house in a new-to-me neighborhood. Electric heat, not gas. Fireplace but no firewood. Near-zero lows were predicted. How would I survive? My phone rang. It was my friend Julie from church. She lived just around the block. "I have gas logs," she said. "Come on over."

Night was falling as I gingerly made my way to Julie's house. When she opened the door, I burst into tears. "I thought I might freeze to death!" I wailed. Next to the blazing fire was a plate of peanut butter sandwiches, plus an oil lamp, a deck of cards, and two mattresses piled high with blankets.

And a soon-to-be best friend who made two frigid days in winter one of the happiest memories of my life.

—Jennie

I'm forever grateful, Lord, for friends. Amen.

renew

Inside myself is a place where I live all alone and that
is where I renew my springs that never dry up.
—Pearl S. Buck

I recently moved to the southern Nevada desert. Having never before lived in such a climate, I wasn't sure what to expect. I've learned a lot. One of the things that has amazed me is the effect a tiny rainfall can have on the area. It's delightful to see a brown-and-gray, rocky expanse of landscape turn green overnight after a sprinkling of rain.

I've known dry periods and desert stretches in my life, and I probably haven't seen the last of them. I'm comforted, though, with the knowledge that even a tiny prayer like "renew a steadfast spirit within me" (Ps. 51:10 NIV) can quickly turn my heart into a garden of God's goodness and grace.

—Bob

*Restore us to Yourself, Lord, that we may return;
renew our days as of old (Lam. 5:21 NIV). Amen.*

unbelief

"'If you can'?" said Jesus. "Everything is possible for one who believes." Immediately the boy's father exclaimed, "I do believe; help me overcome my unbelief!"
—Mark 9:23–24 NIV

love this intimate, heartfelt exchange between a desperate dad and Jesus. How often have I cried out to God for deliverance, unable to believe He would act on my behalf? I can almost hear Jesus's forehead-smacking frustration with the man's question, as if to say, "Of course I can, if you'd just believe!" Still, we don't always receive the rescue we hope for, yet God still invites us to entrust the outcome to Him. My baby wasn't delivered from a Down syndrome diagnosis, but he's the best gift ever. My marriage didn't survive, but I see blessing in both its tenure and its demise. My friend did have cancer, but the illness revolutionized her faith. True faith is much more complex and powerful than the easy answer.

—Isabella

Lord, I believe. Help my unbelief. Amen.

awe

May the heavens be joyful, and may the earth rejoice;
may the sea roar, and all it contains.
—Psalm 96:11 NASB

Commercial diving is tough work, but you get to see some of the most incredible sights on the planet. Seventy feet down an oil rig leg, the crystal-clear, sun-drenched water suddenly went dark. I turned. A *massive* wall of small fish, as far as I could see from the surface to the deep, blocked every bit of light. Then, with a swirl, a hole opened in the wall, making way for an elephant seal the size of a horse. He cruised through, feeding, then turned and passed through again. Over and over. I hung there in the blue and watched, in awe, spellbound, while God put on a show I'll never ever forget.

What a God I serve! He colors the cosmos and guides the stars, but still takes time to tell me He loves me with awesome wonders.

—Buck

God, thank You for delighting in delighting me! Amen.

instruction

She speaks with wisdom, and faithful instruction is on her tongue.
—Proverbs 31:26 NIV

A text pings my phone. *The coffee bar is open.* The coffee bar is a Keurig machine, and the text is from my friend Pat, an octogenarian who schedules our weekly coffee dates. Depending on the weather, we sit on her back porch or in her sunroom and talk about family, the past, books, our ministries and prayer. She helped me through the loss of my mother and prayed us through my husband's leukemia battle. She's been wise counsel as my children prepared to leave the nest and provided faithful instruction as I seek my purpose in this new stage of life. She taught me how a prayer warrior defeats the enemy and just how true God's Word is. Even in the busiest of weeks, I make time to receive instruction from my wise and faithful friend.

—Karen

Father, thank You for blessing me with a friend whose instruction I know is from You. Amen.

roots

Deep in their roots, all flowers keep the light.
—Theodore Roethke

Yesterday I asked the man who takes care of my lawn to mow down the ox-eye daisies. They brought me such joy last spring, with their brilliant white petals and bright-yellow centers. These "He loves me, he loves me not" daisies grow wild in the ditches where I live. Years ago, I dug some up and transplanted them to a sunny spot in my yard so I could have an easy-to-pick fresh bouquet on my table in April and May.

When the hot summer sun wilts the daisies, I chop off their pitiful heads with my hedge trimmers. Now, as fall becomes winter, it's time the daisies were mowed down to be even with the brown grass. But the daisies aren't really gone. I know that, underground, their roots are spreading, preparing bouquets for my table when spring rolls around again.

—Jennie

Thank You, Lord, for daisies, which remind me that light always overcomes darkness. Amen.

somebody

Before I formed you in the womb I knew you,
before you were born I set you apart.
—Jeremiah 1:5 NIV

It used to be easy for me to get caught up in comparing myself and my life to others. All I had to do was go on social media and I'd get sucked into the vortex of people who are more successful or popular, prettier or smarter—and I always wound up not feeling good about myself. Recently I've stopped playing the comparison game and decided that I exist as somebody who's unique and talented in my own way—just like everyone else is unique and talented in their own way too. Why compare when we are each somebody special?

—Jaylin

Lord, thank You for making me somebody unique, beautiful, talented, smart, friendly, and so much more. Amen.

mend

He heals the brokenhearted and binds up their wounds.
—Psalm 147:3 NIV

I have a handful of silvery scars on my face—the result of several basal cell skin cancer surgeries and a childhood injury. While I still occasionally wish my complexion weren't marred, I've begun to look at my scars as evidence of healing and wholeness, proof that the problem has been remedied. The scars make me grateful for the surgeons who carefully stitched me back together, mending my wounds.

Though not outwardly visible, I also carry similar emotional scars. They, too, are evidence of healing, of God having removed the blemishes of my wrongdoings and other painful experiences I've endured. Though I will unfortunately encounter hardships that wound me, and though I have spiritual cancers that must be removed, I can trust Him to mend my heart with His perfect love and tender care.

—Kirsten

Thank You, Father, for being a loving surgeon who mends my wounds. Amen.

gather

*For where two or three gather in my name,
there am I with them.*
—Matthew 18:20 NIV

When my husband, Scott, and I planted our church fifteen years ago, we decided to call our church meetings "gatherings" instead of "services." Scott's thought was that, according to Jesus, the church was a group of people, not a meeting time in a building. Every Sunday our church (the people) would gather and invite Jesus to come be with us. To hear us praise His name. To speak His truth to our hearts. To change. Our gathering was an invitation for His presence. There is something powerful about rubbing elbows with others who love Jesus. Those moments of connection encourage me, refocus my heart, and assure me that Jesus is on the move. When I gather with others, I am in the presence of the One Who loves me most of all.

—Susanna

*Lord, as I gather with those who love You, remind me
that You are always with me. Amen.*

overflow

Now unto him that is able to do exceeding abundantly above all that we ask or think, according to the power that worketh in us.
—Ephesians 3:20 KJV

When two large Memphis churches announced, "Love Thy Neighbor," an initiative to address divisions in the city, I was beyond excited. The hope was to establish ongoing connections between the congregations. The main event was a joint worship service in Memphis's Pyramid Arena that would take place Easter morning.

Rev. Dr. Martin Luther King Jr.'s assassination in 1968 left Memphis ripe to receive the effort in 1997. The two congregations (one mostly black, one mostly white) would be hosts. The community was invited. As cochairpersons, a friend and I helped implement the initiative and led a team of several hundred volunteers. Collectively, we prayed and planned for twelve thousand to come.

We experienced an overflow! More than sixteen thousand attended the service! The overabundance of people—and love—renewed my faith in harmony even when there are differences.

—Steve

Thank You, Lord, for overflow. Amen.

stay

To hold a man down, you have to stay down with him.
—Booker T. Washington

I consider myself loyal. The flip side is that I can hold a mean grudge. When I noticed that a friend had long since moved on from a tiff with a mutual friend—but I couldn't let it go—I realized I was conflating loyalty with unforgiveness. "You can't stay angry," she told me. "You have to move on."

For much of my life I've considered the ability to remain, or stay the course, as a positive thing. After all, it showed I was loyal, dedicated, and enduring. But sometimes it meant I was unrelenting, obsessed, and unwilling to, well, move on. Now I've learned that there are friendships and moments that I need to stay in, and others that I need to let go, and I'm all the better for knowing the difference.

—Ashley

Lord, help me to stay where You need me
and to move when the time is right. Amen.

what

We do not know what to do, but our eyes are on you.
—2 Chronicles 20:12 NIV

A friend of mine died recently. Another friend faces a crucial health decision. Another is recovering from a severe auto accident, while yet another struggles with a wayward child. At such times, it's natural to ask "Why?" It seems like a reasonable question, but I choose not to pray it. Instead, I pray "What?"

I think it's a question God is far more likely to answer than "Why?" Not "God, I want an explanation," but "God, what should my response to this be?" "What now?" "What next?" "What can I do to help?" "What are you teaching me? Showing me? Making of me?"

You may still find it impossible not to ask "Why?" Who knows, maybe you'll get an answer. But it may be better to let "Why?" lead to the better question: "What?"

—Bob

God, when I don't understand "why," help me to trust You and focus on "what." Amen.

wild

I come into the peace of wild things who do not tax
their lives with forethought of grief.
—Wendell Berry, "The Peace of Wild Things"

Two months after my dog died, a groundhog began hanging out in the drainage pipe that runs across my front yard. Then I spotted a doe and her fawn grazing in the backyard next to the woods. Best of all, a red fox took up residence in the brush pile near my garage. Though I didn't name the groundhog or the deer, I call the fox Ginger. None of these animals are pets, of course, but that doesn't lessen the pleasure I get from them being near. Early every morning, I take a steaming mug of coffee out to my porch and settle into the swing to watch for them.

And—for a while, at least—I feel no despair, no fear, no grief. The peace of wild things permeates my soul.

—Jennie

*I'm grateful for all Your creatures, Lord,
be they wild or domesticated. Amen.*

surrender

I have been driven many times upon my knees by the overwhelming conviction that I had no where else to go.
—Abraham Lincoln

On the carbine-and-cannons battlefield, surrender looks like being outgunned, cornered, and out of options. It looks a lot like defeat. On the battlefield of faith, surrender isn't really all that different. I've been there quite a few times. I've fought with all my limited strength to gain victory over a sin, a troubled relationship, a problem I ultimately couldn't fix. It was too big and baffling for me to conquer. I imagine my Heavenly Commander watching and waiting, knowing I would ultimately raise my hands in surrender. Unlike our earthly opposition, this Captor is kind, merciful, and gracious. As soon as I fall to my knees, He extends a hand of rescue, delivering me from the ultimate defeat of death and despair.

—Isabella

Savior, save me from my misguided efforts to fight losing battles and rather to surrender to your loving captivity. Amen.

legacy

Legacy is not leaving something for people.
It's leaving something in people.
—Peter Strople

One day when my sister and I got home from school, my mother said, "Don't go upstairs. Your dad's upset. His brother died in a car accident this afternoon."

"Daddy had a brother?"

Years earlier, my dad and his brother had argued and hadn't spoken since. Now his brother was dead, and my father was heartbroken.

Daddy changed immediately. Days later, he rededicated his life to the Lord and our family joined a church. Sunday service replaced eighteen holes of golf. Daddy became more thoughtful, but the biggest change was that he started to say "I love you." Words he couldn't say to his brother, he could say to my mom, my sisters, and me. And we could say them to him.

Soon, "I love you" supplanted "goodbye" at the end of our family's conversations.

Daddy's gone now, but his legacy of love remains in us.

—Janet

Dear Lord, thank You for love. Amen.

skip

Lou, Lou, skip to my Lou,
Skip to my Lou, my darling.
—Children's song

M y granddaughter Josephine was a late walker. But when she finally learned, there was no stopping her. Because she lives a long plane ride away from me, I didn't get to see her take her first steps. By the time I was finally able to visit, she'd learned something equally as wonderful as walking. Skipping!

Child development experts postulate that, as children gain balance and agility, they spontaneously begin skipping. Perhaps it's to keep up with adults who have much longer strides. Skipping, after all, covers ground more quickly than walking. Some experts say skipping is nature's way of strengthening children's skeletons. I say there's another, and much more delightful, reason why children skip. It's an expression of pure joy. Next time I visit joyful Josephine, we're going to hold hands and skip all the way down the sidewalk together.

—Jennie

Heavenly Father, grant that I may never grow too old or too dignified to skip. Amen.

hush

A hush is over everything, Silent as women wait for love.
—Sara Teasdale

The birth of my first child was a serene affair. She arrived in the world calm and composed. Her younger brother, however, was born kicking and screaming. So, my first conversation with him consisted of one word, exclusively and repeatedly: "Hush."

It's not hard to imagine that the word (or its Aramaic equivalent) was also one of Mary's or Joseph's first prayers to Jesus, as they "wrapped him in cloths and placed him in a manger" (Luke 2:7 NIV). It seems as certain and as fitting as everything else we know about that strange and wonderful night. Two thousand years later, the single syllable "hush" (or "shhh") can be turned into a reminder to our own souls, a plea for calm and quiet amid all the tumult, all the distractions, that tend to crowd out the music and beauty of our Savior's presence.

—Bob

Lord, hush my heart, mind, and soul and let me hear Your gentle whispers. Amen.

bridge

Only Christ could build a bridge to God with
only two pieces of wood.
—Asahel Nettleton

My touristy stroll across the Brooklyn Bridge was the highlight of my trip to New York. Completed in 1883, the iconic bridge still spans the East River, connecting the people of Brooklyn to Manhattan with both speed and ease. As I marveled at the structure, I was reminded that while there are other ways to cross a river, there's only one way for us to have our broken connection to God restored: Jesus. Through His sacrifice on the cross, Jesus became the bridge we needed, spanning the distance between us and God. Because of Jesus, we can walk with God and enjoy being in His presence.

—Kirsten

*Thank You, Jesus, for being my bridge to God. Help me
become a "bridge builder" for others to know You. Amen.*

stories

Life is a book, and there are a thousand pages
I have not yet read.
—Cassandra Clare

Where would I be without a good story? My obsession with books is something few understand. I have read a thousand stories and lived a thousand lives thanks to books. Nothing gives me as much joy as a good story. My emotions end up on a roller coaster. I feel the characters' happiness as well as their pain. Once I ranted to a friend about how upset I was about an ending of a book and when I stopped to catch my breath, she pointed out, "Isn't that the goal of an author? To make you, the reader, *feel* something?" She was right. I get lost in a book to the point that I feel as if I am right there with the characters, exploring new worlds. It's the best form of escapism.

—Sabrina

Thank You, Lord, for stories, both real and fictional. Amen.

SOW

He who sows sparingly will also reap sparingly, and he who sows bountifully will also reap bountifully.
—2 Corinthians 9:6 NKJV

When I graduated from college and got my first job, I felt like an adult. When it was time to pay the bills, I missed being a college student who had no bills! But I'm grateful that my mother taught me and my siblings about sowing and reaping and the importance of tithing when we were very young. If someone gave me money for any reason, I knew to give a portion of it to the church. My mother said, "If you give into God's hands, He'll multiply it much better than you can."

Over the years, I've continued to practice the principle of sowing and reaping, even in other areas of my life. This principle hasn't failed me. When I plant a good seed, I reap a good harvest—and it's always greater than the seed sown.

—Rosalind

Father, thank You for an abundant harvest. Amen.

eternal

If I take up the wings of the dawn, if I dwell
in the remotest part of the sea.
—Psalm 139:9 NASB

The sun sets, brilliant above the horizon line. The tall sails above me fade from brilliant fire to dull gold, then shadow. Soon the night will come in earnest. Later, a sunrise. A cycle as old as time. And as fresh as those first joy-filled words—*Let there be light!*

The sea is immense, endless. To the Great Captain, it's a drop of dew on a mast shroud. To me, the never-ending cycle of night and day feels eternal. To Him, it's a half tick of the second hand.

Because He *is* eternal.

I sail on until, sailor-tired, the harbor takes me in.

As I tie up my boat, stars hang around me, a silent testament to His glory.

Yes, He is eternal. And because He is, *so am I.*

Because I am loved.

—Buck

Lord, the sea is great, my boat is small, but You are eternal, You are all. Amen.

restore

I will restore to you the years that the swarming
locust has eaten.
—Joel 2:25 NKJV

A severe storm raged through our community and damaged parts of our home's roof. Though money was extremely tight in our household, we paid a friend to repair the sections that needed immediate attention while we filed an insurance claim. We soon discovered that the whole roof needed to be replaced. The insurance company balked, claiming that the repairs had negated the policy. We prayed desperately for a resolution and, after many delays, the insurer paid the claim.

Less than two years later, we were packing for a long-distance move and looked back on the ordeal. Though a storm and a recalcitrant insurer had caused much anguish, God not only answered our prayers, but also provided a new roof that made our decades-old home much easier to sell. We had prayed for Him to restore what had been lost; He did that and more.

—Bob

Father, restore years, losses, hopes, dreams, and more. Amen.

call

What a man can be, he must be.
This need we call self-actualization.
—Abraham Maslow

We each have a calling God picked for us before time (Eph. 2:10). I believe our calling is to express Him and His love in the unique way He designed each of us to do. Not one call is greater or lesser than any other. In this light, it would seem easy to discern His call on my life, but it has been anything but. My dear but broken parents couldn't affirm my unique gifts or give me a place to grow them in safety and love. Our world distorts our calling, valuing one over another with a price tag. Religion can distort calling by demonizing some as unholy. God's call doesn't fit neatly in our little boxes. At fifty-three, I'm only now really discerning my calling, which absolutely begins by being most fully myself as an ambassador of God's love.

—Isabella

Papa, help me discern my true calling in Your loving, creative voice. Amen.

abba

Because we are his children, God has sent the Spirit of his Son into our hearts, prompting us to call out, "Abba, Father."
—Galatians 4:6 NLT

Yes, Abba is a Swedish rock band with hits like "Mamma Mia."

It is also an ancient Aramaic word that means Father, but a more intimate form of address, like Daddy.

When I *really* wanted something from my father, I'd end my plea with "*Please, Daddy?*" in a voice that I did my best to make irresistible. Usually, I saw my father's eyes soften as he agreed to grant my wish. How could he say no?

When Jesus really wanted God's attention, He would call His Father *Abba.*

And Jesus told us to do the same. After all, what father can resist an expression of utter love, reliance, and confidence that all will be well as long as Daddy is in charge?

Today when you pray, try addressing God as Abba.

—Michelle

Dear Abba, thank You for being Daddy as well as Father. Amen.

reap

For whatever a man sows, that he will also reap.
—Galatians 6:7 NKJV

I n March, I scattered some lettuce seeds in a flowerpot filled with dirt and sprinkled them with water. I put the pot in a sunny spot on my deck and—voilà—just a few weeks later I had homegrown salad greens. They were delicious. But hot summer temperatures burned up my lettuce and, though I meant to plant flowers in the pot, I never got around to it. Imagine my surprise when, in October, I discovered lettuce growing again! It was just as prolific and delicious as my spring crop.

I love the biblical warning about reaping what we sow, though I always assumed it meant big things. Discord or harmony. Selfishness or generosity. Lies or truth. But now I relish the thought that maybe the Bible is also talking about sowing and reaping little things.

Lettuce, for instance.

—Jennie

Father, help me to sow good things so that I may reap good things. Amen.

glory

I consider our present sufferings insignificant compared to
the glory that will soon be revealed to us.
—Romans 8:18 GW

My husband, Kevin, and I have pastored churches
for forty-plus years. We've heard many people say,
"When I get to heaven, I'm going to ask Jesus (*you
name it*)." One Sunday over dinner I said, "What are you going
to ask Jesus when you meet Him face to face?" Kev's tone was
serious. "I don't think anyone will ask Him questions for a while,
Jeanette. We'll be flat on our faces, worshipping the One Who
gave us eternal life." *Aha*, I thought, *I believe Kevin's right*. All
our pain and anguish will disappear in an instant. Jesus's glory,
splendor, and beauty will fill and spill over the boundaries
of our hearts and heaven's walls. Worship will be the natural
response.

—Jeanette

*God, help me show Your glory in my life here on earth,
so others will see how spectacular You are. Amen.*

perfection

There is no fear in love; but perfect love casteth out fear.
—1 John 4:18 KJV

For three decades I worked as a stylist for home décor publications. In those days, I abhorred imperfection and usually sought out props with no visible flaws. I guess I feared that less-than-perfect objects would make *me* look less than perfect.

I recently came across an enchanting vintage teapot I'd once used in a photo shoot. A friend had given it to me, and I'd featured it to celebrate her. Tucked inside the teapot's handle was the magazine photo in which it appeared. At first glance it seemed picture-perfect. But it actually had more issues than I did! The spout had a chip, and its side bore a sizable crack. As I celebrated our friendship, I saw that teapot with eyes of love. Its flaws were perfectly imperfect, just like the two of us.

—Roberta

Keep the lens of my heart ever focused on Your love, Lord. You're the only source of perfection in this world. Amen.

winning

The big thing is to make a winning effort.
I'm not obsessed with wins.
—Morgan Wootten

Understandably, my heart was bursting with excitement! My wife and I were working hard to keep our cheering and applause the perfect balance of enthusiasm and encouragement without causing embarrassment. Our son had just received the defensive player award from his recreation league basketball team. The award recognized more than just pure basketball skill. It placed a premium on effort, drive, and sportsmanship. Our son was approaching middle school and we were teaching him life lessons and applications beyond sports. Yes, performance and competition were important, but this acknowledgment served as a great reinforcement of our approach—that our son's best effort was more important than winning.

—Steve

*Dear Lord, please help me to give my best,
winning effort in everything I do. Amen.*

longing

The desire is thy prayers; and if thy desire is without ceasing,
thy prayer will also be without ceasing. The continuance of
your longing is the continuance of your prayer.
—St. Augustine

As a mom, I am experiencing a new type of longing. My
son, Jack, just completed his freshman year of college.
He is staying in California this summer, having fun,
spending time with friends, and planning for next year. I am
happy for him, but I miss him. I have a deep longing to hug
his neck. Since that isn't possible, I am turning my longing into
prayer. God knows and loves Jack. With prayer, I can release my
heart's longing into the loving arms of the One Who protects,
saves, and provides. My longings for peace, for joy, for contentment, and healing are safe in the arms of the One Who loves
me most of all.

—Susanna

*God, I give You the longings of my heart. Thank You
for taking care of all of my needs. Amen.*

parable

Every perfect life is a parable invented by God.
—Simone Weil

I love parables. Jesus used these simple stories to teach spiritual truths to sometimes obstinately dense mortals. On my best days, when I'm serene and attentive and curious, I see Jesus orchestrating situations and encounters that impart spiritual truth in my life. In fact, most of my Guideposts writings are simple stories from my life that illustrate spiritual truth to me and others. As a woman who can overcomplicate absolutely anything, I cherish the gift of seeing God's hand in both mundane moments and the larger tapestry of my life. Over time, I've learned to look expectantly for Jesus in everything and everyone in my life. I remind myself that simple understanding and faith is what God wants for me.

—Isabella

Dear Jesus, help me see the parable You are writing with my life. Help me learn and share the wisdom I glean from You! Amen.

invest

Put your life, your time, your money, your talent,
put everything you've got in Christ.
—William Marrion Branham

I worried our investment wouldn't pay off. The real estate market in our new hometown wasn't doing well. We'd left our families so my husband could take a new job, and the house purchase made it feel even riskier because my husband and I might not get our savings out of it later. I relate it to the disciples who feared their investment in Jesus might not pay off. They had left their homes, jobs, and families for Him. But Jesus encouraged them to not fear, assuring them that anyone willing to sacrifice for Him would receive much in return (Mark 10:30). I know that when I invest my life in God, what I get back isn't measured in dollars and cents, but in the joy that comes from knowing Him now and forever!

—Kirsten

Jesus, I put my life into Your hands. Thank You for the joy it is to walk with You through life. Amen.

could

We could never learn to be brave and patient
if there were only joy in the world.
—Helen Keller

---

knew exactly what I wanted to do: write. Unfortunately, that turned out to be the easy part. Now I was tasked with figuring out how to get a foot in the door of a bustling industry. I had stacks of applications ready to be sent out, but the possibility that everyone would reject me was preventing me from actually putting the applications in the mail. "You're only thinking about what could go wrong," my roommate said one day. "What about what could go right?" In that moment, the word *could* stood out. Suddenly I realized that I'd been focused on only the negative possibilities, never considering the flip side of the coin. I have now spent fourteen years in the publishing industry, and still I counsel coworkers to focus on what *could* be, not what *might* fail.

—Ashley

Lord, open my eyes to the possibilities all around me. Amen.

serendipity

Sometimes serendipity is just intention unmasked.
—Elizabeth Berg

I was really looking forward to taking a picture of the New York City skyline. After years of dreaming, and detours to Fort Hood, Texas and Iraq thanks to the army, I was finally moving to the Big Apple. I was starting graduate school at New York University on my thirty-third birthday. Serendipity helped pieces of the move fall into place—an army buddy's second room would be free just when I needed it. And did I want to buy her roommate's practically new bed? The night of the move I didn't get to take the quintessential skyline photo, because I was driving, but my mom and I not only found a legal parking spot in front of my new apartment building, but I also didn't have to parallel park either. Serendipity indeed!

—Allison

Heavenly Father, I know You have a hand in events that feel like serendipity. Thank You for meeting my needs before I can name them. Amen.

WOW

This is too much, too wonderful—I can't take it all in!
—Psalm 139:6 MSG

I had the joy recently of taking my wife to see the Grand Canyon for the first time in her life. As we stood on the South Rim and gazed at one of the natural wonders of the world, she (who usually has plenty to say on any subject) said only, "Wow!" I'm sure it's a common response to that sight.

"Wow" is often a form of prayer. It contains elements of thanks and praise, of surprise and wonder. When a hummingbird peeks in a window. When a sunset paints the sky. When a friend reaches out in self-sacrificing kindness. When a perfect sentence in a book takes your breath away. When a newborn grips your finger. "Wow" is a natural response to something supernatural.

—Bob

God, thank You for the "wow" moments I've experienced—and those yet to come. Amen.

notes

day 11

Make me want again to be holy.

Thomas Merton quote from his journals, August 2, 1960, IV.28.

day 13

Bloom in all Thy beauty in the garden of my heart. Sidney Edward Cox, "In the Garden of My Heart," public domain. Initially published in The Salvation Army's *The Musical Salvationist* in London, September 1940.

day 38

Be here, be now.

Quote from Reynolds Price, "Hymn," from The Collected Poems (New York: Scribner, 1997), 243.

day 66

Blot out, correct, insert, refine. Enlarge, diminish, interline.

Quote from Jonathan Swift's "On Poetry," lines 85–88.

day 253

"Hide me, O my Savior, hide, Till the storm of life is past." Lyrics by Charles Wesley, "Jesus, Lover of My Soul," public domain.

day 302

I need to listen, listen for the prayer of God that is rising in my heart, perhaps for the prayer that I should be praying rather than the one that I am praying.

Quote from Robert Benson, Living Prayer (New York: Tarcher/Putnam, 1998), 134.

reflections

reflections

reflections

reflections

reflections

reflections

reflections

reflections

reflections

a note from the editors

We hope you enjoyed *Pray a Word a Day*, published by Guideposts. For over 75 years, Guideposts, a nonprofit organization, has been driven by a vision of a world filled with hope. We aspire to be the voice of a trusted friend, a friend who makes you feel more hopeful and connected.

By making a purchase from Guideposts, you join our community in touching millions of lives, inspiring them to believe that all things are possible through faith, hope, and prayer. Your continued support allows us to provide uplifting resources to those in need. Whether through our communities, websites, apps, or publications, we inspire our audiences, bring them together, and comfort, uplift, entertain, and guide them.

To learn more, please go to guideposts.org.

We would love to hear from you:

To make a purchase or view our many publications, please go to shopguideposts.org.
To call us, please dial (800) 932-2145
Or write us at Guideposts, P.O. Box 5815, Harlan, Iowa 51593

Made in the USA
Columbia, SC
14 December 2024